NELSON
MANDELA

Read this other REAL-LIFE STORY

Sally Ride: Life on a Mission

A REAL-LIFE STORY

NELSON
MANDELA

SOUTH AFRICAN REVOLUTIONARY

by BEATRICE GORMLEY

ALADDIN

New York   London   Toronto   Sydney   New Delhi

ALADDIN

An imprint of Simon & Schuster Children's Publishing Division

1230 Avenue of the Americas, New York, New York 10020

First Aladdin hardcover edition April 2015

For information about special discounts for bulk purchases, please contact

Simon & Schuster Special Sales at 1-866-506-1949 or business@simonandschuster.com.

The Simon & Schuster Speakers Bureau can bring authors to your live event.

For more information or to book an event contact the

Simon & Schuster Speakers Bureau at 1-866-248-3049 or

visit our website at www.simonspeakers.com.

Book designed by Karina Granda

The text of this book was set in Bembo.

Manufactured in the United States of America 0315 FFG

2 4 6 8 10 9 7 5 3 1

Library of Congress Cataloging-in-Publication Data

Gormley, Beatrice.

Nelson Mandela : South African revolutionary / by Beatrice Gormley. —

First Aladdin hardcover edition

p. cm. — (A real-life story) Includes bibliographical references and index.

1. Mandela, Nelson, 1918–2013—Juvenile literature. 2. Presidents—South Africa—

Biography—Juvenile literature. I. Title.

DT1974.G67 2014

968.06'5092—dc23

[B]

2014019020

ISBN 978-1-4814-2059-4 (hc)

ISBN 978-1-4814-2061-7 (eBook)

To my college classmate
Ifeanyi A. Menkiti

CONTENTS

CHAPTER 1

A VILLAGE HERD-BOY

ON AN ISLAND OFF THE COAST OF SOUTH AFRICA, A tall, thin man with graying hair sat in his prison cell. It was 1975. Nelson Mandela was fifty-seven, and he had lived in this cell, which measured seven feet by eight feet, for eleven years. Now he stared at the small barred window in front of him and called up scenes from his childhood.

In his mind's eye, Mandela saw a landscape of rolling green hills. A small boy in an orange blanket appeared on one hilltop, driving cattle with a switch. Mandela seemed to smell roasting corn and taste milk fresh from the cows. He seemed to watch the flames in the fire pit as he listened to his mother's voice, telling ancient folktales to him and his sisters.

Mandela began to write the story of his life.

• • •

Nelson Mandela was born in a thatched hut in the village of Mvezo, on the banks of the Mbashe River, on July 18, 1918. His mother was Nosekeni Fanny Nkedama, the third wife of the village chief, Gadla Henry Mphakanyiswa of the Mandela family. They belonged to the Thembu, one of several tribes in the Transkei region of South Africa who spoke the Xhosa language. They named their baby boy Rolihlahla, which literally means "pulling the branch of a tree." It is also an expression meaning "troublemaker."

The year of Rolihlahla's birth, 1918, was the year that World War I ended in Europe. Also in 1918 a new South African organization, the African National Congress (ANC), sent a delegation to the Versailles peace conference in France. The ANC was protesting the unfair treatment of black South Africans, because the Union of South Africa had been created in 1910 with no black representatives in the government. The founders of the ANC hoped that by banding together instead of fighting each other, the tribes of South Africa could protect their rights. But in 1918 and for many years afterward, the protests of the ANC were ignored.

By the time of Rolihlahla's birth, the Transkei, a section of the Eastern Cape of South Africa, was no longer ruled by the Xhosa tribes themselves. The British had seized control of the Cape early in the nineteenth century, and in the following decades they continued to struggle with the Dutch settlers, called "Boers," for the remaining territories of South Africa. Therefore the British were more concerned about working out an agreement with the Boers than about protecting the rights of the native tribes. In 1910 the Boer-controlled lands joined the British-controlled lands to form the Union of South Africa, a dominion in the British Empire.

Meanwhile, the Thembu and other Xhosa were allowed to live in the Transkei, but they did not own the land. They paid rent to the British government. The chiefs and elders had a certain amount of power in their own villages, but the final authority in the Transkei was the all-white government of the Union of South Africa.

Several months after Rolihlahla's birth, a villager in Mvezo went to the local white magistrate, protesting a decision the chief had made about a stray ox. The magistrate summoned Gadla Henry to appear before him. Gadla Henry refused, feeling that his authority as chief of the village should be respected. But the magistrate would not allow *his* authority to be defied. He removed Gadla Henry from the chieftainship, and he took away his herd of cattle and his land.

His wealth gone, Gadla Henry could no longer support such a large family. Nosekeni Fanny took her baby, Rolihlahla, and moved from Mvezo to Qunu, a village in a valley thirty miles to the north. Her relatives and friends there helped her set up her *kraal*, a fenced yard with three *rondavels,* round huts. The huts were made of mud bricks, and their grass thatch roofs were supported by a pole in the middle. There was no furniture except sleeping mats, no floors except hard-packed dirt. One hut was for cooking, one for sleeping, and one for storage.

By custom, Gadla Henry traveled among each of his four wives and their children, now separated by many miles. He spent about one week every month in Qunu. He was stern with his children, as was the custom among the Thembu.

Rolihlahla admired his tall, dark, dignified father and wanted to be like him. In fact, he did have his father's high cheekbones and slanting eyes. Since Gadla Henry's black hair grew in a white tuft above his forehead, the young boy tried to copy that look by rubbing white ashes into his hair.

Although Gadla Henry had been stripped of his chieftainship by the white magistrate, he still held a respected position among the Thembu. He was a descendant of the great Thembu king Ngubengcuka, who had united the various Thembu clans in the early nineteenth century. Gadla Henry was not of the royal branch in line to inherit the throne, but he was a counselor to the king of the Thembu. As a respected member of the court, he often traveled with the king and advised him during tribal councils.

Besides their son, Rolihlahla, Gadla Henry and Nosekeni Fanny had three younger daughters: Baliwe, Notancu Mabel, and Makhutswana. Like the other women in Qunu, Nosekeni Fanny grew corn (called "mealies"), beans, sorghum, and pumpkins to feed her family, and she kept her own cows and goats for milk. She cooked in a three-legged iron pot over an open fire.

At the end of the day the family would gather for a supper of "mealie pap," or corn mush, sometimes mixed with milk or beans. Everyone ate from a common dish. After supper, Nosekeni Fanny told the children Xhosa legends and fables.

The people of Qunu lived by the same customs and traditions that had guided village life among the Thembu for many centuries. When a baby was born, the father would slaughter a goat for a feast and hang up its horns in the house. The women and children wore the traditional yellow-orange blanket, wrapped over the shoulder and pinned at the waist. Children were expected to learn by watching and listening, not by asking questions.

In villages like Qunu, people took it for granted that family members could always depend on one another. Rolihlahla grew up thinking of his aunts as mothers, and his cousins as brothers and sisters. The many children of his extended family flowed in and out of the women's *kraals*, cared for by whichever woman or older girl happened to be nearby. The children slept together on mats, sharing blankets.

Another principle of Xhosa life was that people must honor their ancestors. They must learn the tribal history, telling and retelling the old stories for each new generation. Gadla Henry knew Xhosa history especially well. He was a gifted speaker, entertaining listeners with tales of brave Xhosa warriors and fierce battles.

Honoring the ancestors also meant knowing your lineage, tracing it back through many generations. Rolihlahla learned that he belonged to the Madiba clan, named after a

Thembu chief of the eighteenth century. He was a descendant of Ngubengcuka, the last Thembu king to rule free of British supervision, who died in 1832. The family name, Mandela, was inherited from Rolihlahla's grandfather. Even though Gadla Henry and Nosekeni Fanny and their children were now poor, they took a great deal of pride in their heritage.

As a child, Rolihlahla did not wonder why, if his lineage was so noble, his family was so poor. It was simply a fact of life that his family, like almost everyone else in Qunu, had to grow or raise or gather all the food they ate. Even young children needed to do their share of the work. The girls helped their mothers in the *kraal*, fetching water from the streams for cooking and washing and grinding the dry corn between stones to make meal.

The boys were responsible for tending the herds. They drove the cows, sheep, and goats to pasture every morning, watched over them all day, and drove them home and milked them every evening. By the time Rolihlahla was five, he was out in the pastures with the other boys, doing his part.

Day after day on the grassy hillsides, Rolihlahla learned from watching and imitating the older boys. When the boys were hungry, they drank milk straight from the goats and cows. They foraged for wild fruits and honey, and they fished in the many streams flowing through the valley. All their equipment, such as string and a bent wire for fishing, they made themselves.

In between their chores and duties, the children had time to play. A favorite game among the boys of the village was stick fighting. Stick fighting is something like fencing, except that each boy holds two sticks, one to strike with and one to fend off blows. Rolihlahla relished facing an opponent to test his skill at feinting, parrying, and quick footwork. The other boys respected him because Rolihlahla fought to win, but he was careful not to humiliate his opponent.

Rolihlahla and the other boys also rode calves or donkeys, getting tossed off until they learned to stay on. They slid down the large, smooth rocks in the fields, using a smaller flat rock like a sled. Sometimes they played with the girls, and at these times Rolihlahla's favorite game was a flirtatious one called *khetha*, or "choose-the-one-you-like." It was a carefree life for young Rolihlahla. At that time, his highest ambition was to become the best stick fighter in the village.

As for white people, Rolihlahla didn't give them much thought. Qunu was far from the towns and cities of those unfamiliar beings. Only a few whites lived in the area. There was the keeper of the nearby store, where families with a little money bought coffee, tea, and sugar. The local magistrate was white, of course. And once in a while, a white traveler would pass through the village.

Much later, Rolihlahla would realize what a drastic effect the distant white government had on the Africans of Qunu. In 1913, a few years before Rolihlahla's birth, the Natives Land Act had decreed that only 13 percent of the land in the Union of South Africa would be available for black Africans to live on. Hundreds of thousands of black farmers were forced to leave their lands and move to the Transkei.

The Transkei was the largest of the areas reserved for "natives," but it could not support its greatly increased population with farming and herding. The pastures were overgrazed, and the soil became poorer season by season. During Nosekeni Fanny's first years in Qunu, her fields yielded enough corn to supply her family. Later on, the harvest dwindled, and the family had to scrape up the money to buy extra mealie meal. The other villagers suffered the same hardship.

As a result, most of the men of the villages had to look for jobs outside the Transkei. While the women and girls tended the cornfields and the vegetable gardens, and the boys herded the livestock, the men labored on distant farms, or in the mines near Johannesburg. Their work for their white *baas*, or employer, took them so far away that they could come home only once or twice a year.

During Rolihlahla's childhood, the government of South Africa did not provide any education for black Africans. Most of the villagers in Qunu, including Rolihlahla's parents, had no formal schooling and could not read or write. But Gadla Henry had friends, the Mbekela brothers, who had been educated by Methodist missionaries. The Mbekelas were members of another tribe, the Mfengu, who had been driven from their homeland by the Zulu wars of the nineteenth century. Mfengu people were scorned by most Thembus, so it was a sign of Gadla Henry's open mind that he was close to these men.

The Mbekelas persuaded Nosekeni Fanny to be baptized a Methodist, and to wear Western dress rather than the Xhosa blanket. She also had Rolihlahla baptized, although he didn't attend church. As for Gadla Henry, he kept to his traditional faith.

He believed in Qamata, the Great Spirit of his ancestors, and he followed the ancient Xhosa rituals and traditions. In fact, he often acted as priest in the customary
rites for marriages, funerals, harvests, and other important
events in village life. However, Gadla Henry also had great
respect for Western education.

When the Mbekela brothers urged Nosekeni Fanny
to send Rolihlahla to the nearby Methodist school, Gadla
Henry agreed. So at the age of seven, Rolihlahla became
the first person in his family to receive a Western education. On his first day, walking over the hill from the village
to the one-room schoolhouse, Rolihlahla was proud of
the way he was dressed. The family had no money for
new clothes, but Gadla Henry felt that his son should wear
trousers, rather than the traditional Xhosa blanket. He gave
Rolihlahla an old pair of his trousers, cut off at the knees
and gathered around the boy's waist with a piece of string.

The Methodist school offered a British-style education, and it was the custom of the mission-school teachers
to give their African students English names. Rolihlahla's
teacher, Miss Mdingane, told him his name at school
would be "Nelson." She didn't explain why she picked
that name, but later Rolihlahla guessed that she might have

been thinking of the British naval hero Admiral Horatio Nelson. Rolihlahla did well in the little school, learning to read and write in his own language, Xhosa.

Gadla Henry showed his respect for education in his choice for a regent to rule the Thembu tribe. In his role as counselor, he had used his influence to have Jongintaba Dalindyebo appointed acting king, or regent, until the heir to the throne was of age. He had recommended Jongintaba, although he was not the oldest candidate, because he was the best educated.

When Rolihlahla was almost twelve years old, his father arrived in Qunu for the last time, ill with a lung disease. He lay racked with coughs in Nosekeni Fanny's hut for several days. During that time he had a visit from Regent Jongintaba. Gadla Henry asked Jongintaba, head of the Madiba clan, to take Rolihlahla as his ward and educate him. Jongintaba promised to do so.

One night Gadla Henry grew worse. He called for his youngest wife, who was helping to care for him, to bring his pipe, but she and Nosekeni Fanny both felt that smoking would be bad for him. Finally, when he insisted, they brought him the pipe. As Rolihlahla watched, his father smoked his last pipe—and breathed his last breath.

After the funeral and the period of mourning, Nosekeni Fanny told her son to pack his small tin trunk and get ready for a journey. Rolihlahla trusted his mother completely, and he did not ask where he was going or why. At the same time, he sensed that he was leaving not only the village of Qunu, but also the happiest years of his childhood.

The boy and his mother left the village early in the morning. Before the huts of his mother's *kraal* vanished behind the hills, Rolihlahla turned for one last look. They walked all day on dirt roads, up and down hill after hill, following the sun toward the west. Late in the afternoon they arrived at Mqhekezweni, from which Rolihlahla's ancestor Ngubengcuka had ruled the Thembu long ago. This village was still the Great Place, the royal seat, of the Thembu.

In the middle of Mqhekezweni, Nosekeni Fanny stopped in front of a compound grander than any place Rolihlahla had ever seen. The regent and his family lived here in two Western-style houses with tin roofs and six large, well-kept *rondavels*. Lush gardens, orchards, and pastures full of livestock surrounded the dwellings.

A council of tribal elders sat in the shade in front of the

regent's home. As Rolihlahla watched, a shiny motorcar drove up, and a short, thickset man with a thin mustache, wearing a suit, got out. The boy could see that every movement, every gesture of this man expressed confidence and authority. The elders jumped up, shouting, *"Bayete a-a-a, Jongintaba!"* ("Hail, Jongintaba!")

Rolihlahla was overcome with awe: this kingly man was to be *his* guardian. He felt, he said many years later, "like a sapling pulled root and branch from the earth and flung into the center of a stream whose strong current I could not resist." Clearly, from now on his life would be entirely different.

CHAPTER 2
THE GREAT PLACE

A FEW DAYS AFTER ROLIHLAHLA'S ARRIVAL AT Mqhekezweni, his mother left. She would return home, while he stayed in the Great Place as a ward of the regent. Rolihlahla and his mother were close, and she must have been sad to give him up to another family. But she knew this was an extraordinary opportunity for a poor boy from Qunu.

Nosekeni Fanny was matter-of-fact about parting from her son, that day in 1930. She gave him one tender look and said, *"Uqinisufokotho, Kwedini!"* ("Brace yourself, my boy!") Maybe she sensed that the road ahead of him would not always be easy.

Later Rolihlahla would miss his mother, but at the time he was too dazzled with his new home to be sad. How could he need bracing? He was wearing the fine outfit the regent had given him—a new pair of khaki shorts and a new khaki shirt!

Rolihlahla's new clothes were only one of the signs that he was a full member of the regent's family. From the beginning, Jongintaba Dalindyebo and his wife, Nkosikazi No-England, treated Rolihlahla as their son. Their daughter, Nomafu, became his sister, and their son, Justice, became Rolihlahla's older brother. Justice and Rolihlahla shared one of the *rondavels* in the regent's compound.

At the Great Place, even the thatch-roofed *rondavels* seemed luxurious to Rolihlahla. The hut the boys slept in had a wooden floor instead of dirt, real beds instead of mats, and a table with an oil lamp. The village herd-boy was now well-dressed like the regent's children, well-fed with the same food, and treated with respect in Mqhekezweni as the regent's son. It was an enormous change for Rolihlahla, and at first he was shy and silent. Sometimes Rolihlahla looked so serious that his new family gave him the nickname Tatomkhulu, or "Grandpa," because his solemn expression reminded them of an old man.

Regent Jongintaba was strict but fair with his children, now including Rolihlahla. The boy eagerly ran errands for the regent, herded cattle, and milked the cows. One of his chores was pressing the trousers of the regent's suits, and he took pride in this work. Someday, he hoped, he would own a fine suit like one of these.

Rolihlahla looked up to his new brother, Justice, who was four years older and greatly admired in Mqhekezweni. He was tall, handsome, and athletic, with an outgoing personality, and many of the girls had a crush on him. Justice was already attending boarding school at Clarkebury, sixty miles from the Great Place, so he was away much of the time.

While the villagers of Qunu lived much as their Thembu ancestors had always lived, the people of Mqhekezweni had adopted many Western ways. The regent dressed in Western-style suits, and his wife in long skirts and high-necked blouses. They were devout Christians, and Rolihlahla was expected to go to the white stucco Methodist church with them every Sunday.

In these days Rolihlahla was not at all the "trouble-maker" that his Xhosa name implied. He was respectful and hardworking, usually doing without question whatever his foster parents wanted. One Sunday, however, when the boys of Mqhekezweni were meeting the boys of another village for a fight, he sneaked away from church to take part. Afterward, Regent Jongintaba found out and gave Rolihlahla a beating. The boy never skipped church again, as long as he lived in the Great Place.

The worst thing Rolihlahla did was to steal some corn from the garden of the Methodist pastor, carelessly roasting and eating it on the spot. A girl saw him do it, and she told the pastor. Soon everyone in the village, including Rolihlahla's foster mother, No-England, had heard about his theft.

At family prayer time No-England gave him a frightening talking-to. She made Rolihlahla understand that he had shamed his foster family by violating their trust, and he had committed a sin for which the devil would punish him. It was hard to say which was worse.

The pastor, Reverend Matyolo, was an important person in the community, and the Methodist church was packed full every week. The reverend, a heavy man with a deep, powerful voice, preached rousing sermons and led enthusiastic singing. People told stories of Reverend Matyolo's spiritual power—for instance, that he had confronted a dangerous ghost and driven it from the village.

Rolihlahla was very much taken with Reverend Matyolo's younger daughter, Winnie, and she liked him, too. But her older sister thought the boy from Qunu was a country bumpkin, and she tried to discourage Winnie from going out with him. When Rolihlahla came to lunch at the pastor's house one day, the older sister deliberately embarrassed him by serving him a tough chicken wing.

All his life in Qunu, Rolihlahla had eaten sitting on the ground, dipping into the common dish with his fingers. Now he was perched on a chair at a table, watching the others easily wield their knives and forks. Obviously, here it was bad manners to pick up a piece of chicken, so he sweated and sawed away at the gristly wing without getting much meat off the bone. The older sister smiled scornfully, but Winnie liked him just the same. She and Rolihlahla were close for several years, until they both went away to school.

In addition to chores and church, Rolihlahla's new life offered new entertainments. Once in a while, the stern regent allowed the boys to race one another on his horses. Sometimes in the evenings, Rolihlahla and the other boys danced as the young girls sang tribal songs and clapped.

But Rolihlahla understood that Regent Jongintaba had brought him to the Great Place to give him a good education, preparing him to serve as counselor to the next Thembu king. He worked hard at his lessons, and he had an excellent memory. Every day he studied under the corrugated iron roof of the schoolhouse near the church, writing with chalk on a black slate. He did his homework every night, and his aunt Phathiwe checked it for him.

The Mqhekezweni school taught history, geography, reading and writing in the Xhosa language, and English. English was important because it was the official language of South Africa, the language of the white British government, and Rolihlahla made good progress in this subject. One day he and some friends met a white man whose motorbike had broken down, and Rolihlahla was able to speak English with the man and get help for him.

The other children in Mqhekezweni respected Rolihlahla because he was the regent's ward, and also because he was intelligent and did so well in school. However, they sometimes felt that Rolihlahla respected himself a little too much. Perhaps he seemed arrogant because he took the future laid out for him, as tribal counselor, very seriously.

Like all schools for black South Africans, the one near the royal compound was a mission school. The Methodist teachers were African, but they used British textbooks, which gave the impression that the best things in African life came from the British. The textbooks taught that South African history began with the appearance of the first Europeans, the Dutch, in the seventeenth century. Furthermore, the arrival of the British in South Africa in the eighteenth century was a great blessing.

But outside school, Rolihlahla was taking in different lessons. Looking on at the tribal councils, he learned about the Xhosa style of governing. The regent would call a council whenever there was an important matter for the tribe to settle. All the Thembu chiefs were invited to gather at the Great Place for days of discussion and feasting. The other people in the region, rich or poor, were welcome to attend and to take part in the discussions as well.

Rolihlahla listened, fascinated, to the men's debates. He noted which ones spoke well, and how they used reason and emotion to convince their listeners. He also noticed that the regent listened carefully to each speaker, never interrupting even when they criticized him. Jongintaba's style of leadership, never humiliating an opponent or trying to crush him, seemed right and natural to Rolihlahla.

The goal of the tribal council was for the whole

group to come to a satisfactory conclusion, without forcing anyone against his will. When everyone had had a chance to speak, the regent summed up the discussion and pointed out the ways in which everyone agreed. If the council could not agree, there would be another meeting. Jongintaba ruled by the African principle of *ubuntu,* which stressed that everyone in the tribe was bound to everyone else. Harmony in the tribal community was a supreme value.

At the conclusion of a tribal council, the elders would sit around in the dining hall and tell stories of the old days. From the elders, Rolihlahla absorbed a view of South African history that was quite different from that of the British textbooks. These men had a deep knowledge of Xhosa history, going back many generations, to the time before the Xhosa had been conquered by the white invaders.

The elders were master storytellers. They told glorious tales of Xhosa heroes who had triumphed in battle, and tragic tales of Xhosa leaders who had defied the British armies in vain. One leader, Makana, was condemned to life imprisonment on a grim place called Robben Island. He had died trying to escape.

The oldest and most memorable of the storytellers

was Chief Joyi, a descendant of the royal family of Ngubengcuka, like Rolihlahla. The old man was bent over, his withered skin hung in folds, and every so often a loud, wheezing cough interrupted his speech. But when he told stories, people listened, entranced.

Joyi had personally fought in the great chief Ngangelizwe's battles against the British. As he acted out hurling his assegai, or spear, in fierce combat, he seemed to turn into a young warrior again. One of the most thrilled listeners sitting at the elders' feet was Rolihlahla.

Sometimes Chief Joyi praised heroes from other tribes, even traditional enemies such as the Zulu, who lived in a native reserve northeast of the Transkei. The Zulu, the largest ethnic group in South Africa, had nearly wiped out the tribes of the interior of South Africa. Rolihlahla was used to hearing only Thembu heroes praised, and it puzzled him that Joyi had a good word for the Zulu. The old chief seemed to suggest a wider loyalty for all the black tribes, who had lived in South Africa for many centuries before the Europeans arrived.

Chief Joyi accused the white men of deliberately setting Africans against one another and of cheating the Africans out of their land. According to Joyi, before the white men came, all South African tribes were brothers. He denied that the British were the lawful rulers of South Africa, because their rule had broken up the *abantu*, or fellowship, among the tribes. A true ruler took care of his people, but the white man's rule, according to Chief Joyi, had brought only poverty and misery to black Africans. As Rolihlahla listened, he felt hot with anger toward the British.

But Rolihlahla didn't know how to fit together the two opposing versions of history he was learning. He was thrilled by the stories of Xhosa heroes. He wanted to be like these men who were proud and dignified, like his father, even in defeat. At the same time, he was eager to master the ways of the British: their English language, their history, their tailored suits, their table manners. After all, the two most important men in Mqhekezweni, Regent Jongintaba and Reverend Matyolo, were examples of this road to success.

As time went on, Rolihlahla had a chance to see his foster father, the regent, with all kinds of people. In the course of tribal business, the regent dealt with English traders, magistrates, and other white officials. Regent Jongintaba, although not a tall man, had a commanding presence. The boy noticed that the regent was always courteous but dignified, and that others always treated him with respect.

Later Rolihlahla would understand that Jongintaba had made a sort of unspoken bargain with the whites. As far as tribal matters went, the regent was allowed to govern the Thembu without interference. In turn, the regent did not dispute the British control of South Africa. He did not urge his people to fight for fair wages in the mines or the right to vote in South African elections.

While the regent understood how to adopt British ways to deal with the British overlords, he still honored the old traditions. He wanted to have his boys initiated into manhood with the traditional circumcision ritual, as generation upon generation of Thembu boys had always been. In 1934, when Rolihlahla was sixteen, he and Justice, along with twenty-four other youths, traveled to a secret place on the banks of the Mbashe River.

For several days Rolihlahla and the others lived by themselves in two grass huts, playing games and telling stories. Rolihlahla was especially impressed by the stories of a boy who had actually visited the great city of

Johannesburg. In the City of Gold, he claimed, bright electric lights shone on polished motorcars and gorgeous women, and the buildings soared into the sky. According to this boy, the miners of Johannesburg were strong and courageous, performing deeds as heroic as those of the Thembu warriors of yesteryear.

The night before the circumcision ceremony, women came from nearby villages to sing and clap as Rolihlahla and his companions danced. The next morning, the youths bathed in the river in preparation for the noontime event. A crowd of relatives and tribal elders gathered to watch the ceremony, and the circumcision expert appeared with his sharp-bladed assegai.

The ritual was a test of courage, and the boys were not given anything to deaden the pain. Rolihlahla was anxious not to flinch or cry out at the moment of his circumcision, but to endure the test like a man. Each youth was expected to shout bravely, *"Ndiyindoda!"* ("I am a man!")

When Rolihlahla's turn came, he was overwhelmed by the pain for a moment. He managed not to scream, but there was a pause—he was not even sure how long— before he could call out, *"Ndiyindoda!"*

After several more days of healing and ritual body

painting, there was a great celebration to welcome the youths as Thembu men. They received lavish gifts, including cattle and sheep. Rolihlahla was in high spirits, imagining his future as a proud, confident man.

But among the many joyful songs and speeches that day, there was one grim note from Chief Meligqili, a relative of Regent Jongintaba. He spoke of the truth that nobody wanted to hear: The Thembu, like all black South Africans, were a conquered people. For these fine youths, reaching the state of manhood actually meant that they would go to Johannesburg. They would labor in poverty, in white men's mines, to make white men rich.

"We are tenants on our own soil," Meligqili told his unwilling listeners. "We have no strength, no power, no control over our own destiny in the land of our birth." His words made Rolihlahla angry—angry not at the unjust British overlords, but at this speaker who was blighting the youths' special day. Rolihlahla told himself that the chief didn't know what he was talking about.

In fact, Regent Jongintaba had as good as admitted the same thing to his ward. He would never have made a speech as gloomy as Meligqili's in public, but many times he had privately told Rolihlahla, "It is not for you to spend your life mining the white man's gold, never knowing how to write your name." The regent was determined that his own sons, at least, would not suffer the fate of most Xhosa youths. Rolihlahla would be well educated so that, in time, he could take his rightful place as counselor to the new king of the Thembu.

CHAPTER 3

TO BE A "BLACK ENGLISHMAN"

IN 1934 ROLIHLAHLA PREPARED TO LEAVE THE Great Place for boarding school. He had passed the necessary examination, and he had been admitted to the Clarkebury Boarding Institute, the best and largest school in Thembu territory. This was such an important event that Regent Jongintaba gave a celebration in his ward's honor. There was a feast with a whole roast sheep, and singing and dancing. The regent presented Rolihlahla with his first pair of boots, polished to a high shine.

The regent himself drove Rolihlahla southwest to Clarkebury in his splendid Ford V-8. The miles sped by, and Rolihlahla crossed the Mbashe River for the first time. Along the way, Jongintaba advised his ward about what to expect in his new school and how to behave.

The Thembu royal family had a long connection with

Clarkebury, since their ancestor King Ngubengcuka had given the Methodists the land for the school in 1825. The regent had attended Clarkebury himself, as had Justice, and Jongintaba knew and trusted the current headmaster, the Reverend Cecil Harris. Harris was a great friend to the Thembu people, Jongintaba explained. Rolihlahla was to give him every respect and learn from him, and generally act so as to bring honor to the regent and their tribe.

Nelson, as Rolihlahla would be known at school, was deeply impressed by his first sight of Clarkebury. The campus of stately Colonial-style stone buildings spread out on a hillside looked Western, rather than African. Nelson felt that he was entering an unfamiliar world. Clarkebury included the secondary school where he would study, a library, a teachers college, shops for training in trades such as carpentry and printing, separate dormitories for boys and girls, and sports fields.

Regent Jongintaba introduced his ward to Reverend Harris, and for the first time Nelson shook a white man's hand. Nelson was struck with how friendly and warm this important white man was toward the regent. The regent asked for special attention to Nelson, since he would be a tribal counselor one day. Reverend Harris assured

30

Jongintaba that he would take particular care of Nelson.

That first day at Clarkebury, Nelson was feeling rather full of himself. He had recently been initiated into manhood, the whole village of Mqhekezweni had celebrated to send him off to boarding school, and the headmaster had promised to pay him special attention. He was used to respect from the villagers of Mqhekezweni, and he expected that his fellow students would be also be in awe of him. He was not only a descendant of Ngubengcuka, the founder of the school, but also a member of the Thembu royal family.

But Nelson was quickly disappointed. His classmates were also bright students from important families. On the soccer field, they ran faster than Nelson. Many of them, including students from Johannesburg, were more sophisticated than he was. Furthermore, they didn't care that Nelson was a descendant of Ngubengcuka.

The very first day of classes, Nelson got taken down a peg, and it was his shiny new boots that embarrassed him. He was proud of those boots, but he hadn't gotten the hang of walking in them. As Nelson clumped and clattered into the classroom, he noticed a pretty girl in the front row watching him. "The country boy is not used to wearing shoes," she said to her friend, and they laughed. Nelson was so furious, he could hardly see.

In time, however, he became good friends with Mathona, the girl who had made fun of him. She was not only smart and funny, but also someone he could relax with and admit his insecurities to. Sadly, she would not be able to develop her intelligence and talents any further than Clarkebury. Her family didn't have the money to send her on to college, and so that was the end of her education. In later years Nelson would realize how common such a story was among black South Africans, and what a tragic waste of talent that was.

Nelson soon discovered that Reverend Harris ran Clarkebury with strict discipline, almost like a military academy. Harris himself walked like a soldier on parade. He had fought in World War I, when South Africa joined England and the rest of the British Empire to fight against Germany. He was dedicated to educating African youth, and the discipline he expected of his students would serve Nelson well all his life.

The students at Clarkebury were all expected to do some manual work. As a favor to Jongintaba, Reverend Harris assigned Nelson to one of the better jobs, working in his garden. Nelson rather enjoyed tending the head-master's flowers and vegetables; it would be a pleasant memory much later in life, when he was allowed a small garden in prison.

Mrs. Harris, a friendly, chatty woman, often came into the garden while Nelson was doing his chores. Nelson liked her, and he liked the warm buttered scones she brought out to him. He was always hungry, since the school food, like that at many boarding schools, was skimpy and unappetizing.

However, the education at Clarkebury was first-rate. The teachers, black as well as white, were well qualified. Nelson's friend Mathona informed him that their English and history teacher, Gertrude Ntlabathi, had a BA.

Nelson gathered that having a BA must mean a person had achieved a high intellectual level, but he didn't know that it stood for a university degree. When he asked Mathona what exactly a BA was, she answered with authority, "A BA is a very long and difficult book." Nelson would later chuckle over the way Mathona pretended to know, but he was still impressed that the Clarkebury teachers were so well educated.

Even more admirable to Nelson than a BA was the

example of Mr. Mahlasela, a teacher who was not intimidated by Reverend Harris. In South Africa, every black man was expected to show exaggerated respect to every white man, but Mr. Mahlasela always acted as if he and the headmaster were on equal terms. The African students were amazed to see Mahlasela walking into the white principal's office *without removing his hat*, which was the expected form of respect.

Since Nelson had done so well at the Mqhekezweni school, he was taken aback at how challenging his classes at Clarkebury were. Some of the other students were much better prepared. For the first time, he worried about passing his exams. But Nelson studied hard and made good progress. In the end, he managed to graduate from the secondary school in two years rather than the usual three.

Although Clarkebury was mainly a school for Thembu students, it included some students from other parts of South Africa. However, Nelson left Clarkebury still thinking of himself as a proud member of the Thembu tribe, not as a South African. He believed that his Thembu background dictated his fate, and he still expected to become a tribal counselor, as Jongintaba planned.

Nelson was barely aware of developments in the rest of

South Africa, although 1936 was the year that Parliament removed the few black voters in the Cape Province from the general rolls. At the same time Parliament created the Natives Representative Council, a body elected by black voters only. The council was supposed to advise the white government of black Africans' concerns, and they worked hard to do so for the next twelve years. But the white government never paid any attention.

In 1937, at the age of nineteen, Nelson progressed to the Methodist college for elite black students at Healdtown. This school was farther away—175 miles southwest of Mqhekezweni—and in the Ciskei region, a separate native reserve from the Transkei. Healdtown was six miles away from the town of Fort Beaufort, once an actual British fort. The Xhosa warriors about whom Nelson had heard so much had fought many battles with the British nearby.

Located in a beautiful green valley, Healdtown was modeled on English colleges, complete with ivy-covered walls, shady quadrangles, and a clock tower. It was much larger than Clarkebury, with more than a thousand students. On Sundays and special occasions the students wore the full uniform of gray slacks, white shirt, maroon-and-gold-striped

35

tie, and black blazer jacket with a badge and the school's Latin motto. As the British flag was raised and the student brass band played, they sang the British anthem, "God Save the King," as well as "Nkosi Sikelel' iAfrika" ("God Bless Africa"), a South African anthem.

Most of the faculty were British, and the principal was the most British of them all. His name was Dr. Arthur Wellington, and at every assembly he reminded his students that he was a descendant of the famous Duke of Wellington. In 1815 that Wellington had led the British to victory over the French emperor, Napoleon Bonaparte, at the Battle of Waterloo.

When Nelson was older, he would do a wicked imitation of Dr. Wellington's deep, self-important voice. But at the time, Nelson and his fellow students felt privileged to have such a principal. Some Africans might make fun of graduates of Healdtown as "black Englishmen," Africans trying to turn themselves into something they obviously were not. But the students at Healdtown believed, as Dr. Wellington did, that their goal should be to become as English as possible in their education, manners, and ideals.

Nelson never regretted his British-style education, and the discipline he learned at these schools would in the end carry him through seemingly unbearable ordeals. True, Healdtown's heavy emphasis on British history, geography, and literature was a little strange for a school where all the students were African. Nelson learned the geography of the British Isles better than he did the geography of Africa. But in the end, this background would help him bridge the gulf in his country between white and black, Europe and Africa.

Even though Nelson held Dr. Wellington in such high esteem, he was glad to see a black man stand up to him. The housemaster of Nelson's dormitory was Reverend Seth Mokitimi, a popular man who sympathized with the boys. One evening, when Reverend Mokitimi was in the midst of breaking up a quarrel between two senior boys, Dr. Wellington appeared and demanded to know what was going on. The principal was large and overbearing, and the housemaster was a small man. Nevertheless, Reverend Mokitimi calmly assured Dr. Wellington that he was in control and would report to him in the morning.

Dr. Wellington tried to insist on being informed immediately, but the housemaster repeated, politely but firmly, that he would report on the matter tomorrow. To Nelson's astonishment, Dr. Wellington agreed and left the scene.

Nelson stored this incident in his mind together with his observations of Regent Jongintaba and of Mr. Mahlasela at Clarkebury. All these examples showed that it was possible for a black man to maintain his dignity, in a courteous manner, with a white man.

Nelson and his fellow housemates appreciated Reverend Mokitimi's concern for the boys. He tried to institute some reforms in student life at the college. He believed that the students should be given more responsibility for disciplining themselves, and he agreed with their complaints about the food.

For breakfast, the students were served a mug of warm sugar water and a piece of dry bread. Some had enough money to supply their own butter for the bread, but Nelson did not. For lunch, the students ate samp, a corn porridge made with sour milk and beans. On three days during the week, some meat was added to the samp. Dinner was the same as lunch. They ate every meal in the dining hall, under a portrait of George VI, who was the king of England at that time.

Nelson was still working on learning proper British table manners, and he dreaded Sunday lunches, when the male and female students dined together. Struggling with his knife and fork, he never got enough to eat by the time the meal was over.

The schedule at Healdtown was strict, but it did allow time for exercise. Nelson took up long-distance running, which suited his tall, lanky build and allowed him to get away by himself for a space of time. There was not much chance for privacy in his dormitory, where all forty boys slept in one large room, with twenty beds on each side of an aisle. Nelson also tried boxing, but he did not make much progress in that sport.

Nelson did well at Healdtown, and in his second year the principal and the housemaster chose him to be a prefect, or student monitor. This was an honor, but not actually very glamorous. At first Nelson was assigned to supervise students washing windows. Then he was put on night duty, which included making sure that the students used the outhouse behind his dormitory. There was no inside toilet, and in bad weather students were tempted to relieve themselves in the bushes off the veranda.

One very rainy night, Nelson noted down a list of fifteen violators of the outhouse rule. He intended to report all of them, as was his duty. But the next boy to use the bushes was not an ordinary student, but a prefect like Nelson.

The rules of the college said that a prefect could not report another prefect, but Nelson felt this was unfair. The prefect had broken the outhouse rule just as the other fifteen students had. In the end, Nelson decided the only fair thing to do was to not report anyone, and he tore up his list.

The students at Healdtown were not just Thembu, and not only from Xhosa-speaking tribes. There were Sotho speakers from north of the Transkei, and there were even some students from other African countries. However, after classes and on weekends, the young people generally kept to their own tribes.

But Nelson did make one Sotho-speaking friend, Zachariah Molete, which made him feel quite adventurous. Nelson's mind was further broadened when he found out that another Sotho speaker, the popular zoology teacher, was *married* to a Xhosa woman. Nelson had never heard of such an intermarriage.

Impressed as Nelson was with British culture and with all the benefits to be gained from becoming a "black Englishman," he still felt intense pride in his identity as a member of the Thembu tribe and the Xhosa-speaking

40

nation. His history teacher, Weaver Newana, encouraged that side of Nelson by teaching Xhosa history as well as the standard British history. In 1938, Nelson won the school prize for the best essay written in the Xhosa language.

At the end of Nelson's final year at Healdtown, a special visitor came to the college to give an assembly: the Xhosa poet and praise-singer Krune Mqhayi. Mqhayi was famous among the Xhosa-speaking tribes as a passionate oral historian for their people. And he had written several stanzas for "Nkosi Sikelel' iAfrika," the anthem that the students sang every Sunday.

Assemblies were always held in the dining hall, and they always began with Dr. Wellington walking onto the stage through a door at the back of the hall. But on this day, the students watched a black man walk through that same door. Not only that, but a black man wearing a Xhosa leopard-skin *kaross*, or cloak, and carrying an assegai in each hand. Nelson was thrilled to his core.

The appearance of Krune Mqhayi was only the beginning. Besides speaking of Xhosa history, he described a future in which all black Africans would throw off the domination of the white man and re-establish their own culture. Nelson was astonished that Mqhayi, even though he was such a famous poet, dared to speak this way in front of Dr. Wellington.

The day of Mqhayi's visit made a deep mark in Nelson's mind, and yet it added to his already conflicted thoughts. How did the idea of throwing off British domination work with the fact that there were so many benefits to be gained by getting along with white people? How did Nelson's intense loyalty to the Xhosa fit with the idea of joining with other black African peoples to achieve independence?

CHAPTER 4

FUTURE LEADERS

IN 1939, WHEN NELSON MANDELA WAS TWENTY-ONE, HE arrived at the University College of Fort Hare. Like Fort Beaufort near Healdtown, twenty miles away, Fort Hare had once been a British fort defending white settlers against the original Xhosa residents. The campus was set on a plateau overlooking a bend in the Tyhume River.

Only a very few select African students were admitted to Fort Hare. This school offered the best higher education available to blacks in South Africa, or, for that matter, in a good part of the continent of Africa. The student body numbered only 150.

The year before Nelson entered the college, the black American diplomat Ralph Bunche had visited Fort Hare. Bunche noted, "The good native student is the equal of any Indian or Coloured student." He meant that as a compliment, but it underscored the race-conscious attitude of the time.

Fort Hare offered such a good education that black youth from all over Africa came here to study for a degree. They were reminded over and over, by the principal and by their teachers, that they would become the leaders of their people. And in fact, many of the future political leaders of Africa studied at Fort Hare before and after Nelson's time. But they would lead their people in ways that the white authorities did not necessarily expect.

The day Nelson left Mqhekezweni for Fort Hare, he wore his first three-piece suit, a present from Jongintaba. A cousin of Nelson's remembered well how stylish he had looked in that tailored suit. Years later she told an interviewer, "We thought there could never be anyone smarter than him at Fort Hare." Nelson thought the same thing.

The principal at Fort Hare was a Scotsman, Alexander Kerr, with a passionate belief in the education of Africans. The faculty included distinguished black as well as white professors. Z. K. Matthews, a graduate of Fort Hare himself, taught anthropology and native law. The best-known

African professor was Dr. Davidson Jabavu, who taught Latin, Bantu studies, and history, besides directing the college choir. He spoke the Zulu and Sotho languages as well as Xhosa and English. Nelson's own English was rather slow and spoken with a Xhosa accent, and he would speak English that way throughout his life.

The dormitories at Fort Hare were a step up from Healdtown, with flush toilets and hot-water showers. Nelson was expected to adopt some new Western customs, such as wearing pajamas to sleep in. (At first he found pajamas uncomfortable.) He began brushing his teeth with toothbrush and toothpaste, instead of cleaning them with ashes and a toothpick as he had always done.

One of the other residents in Nelson's dormitory was a cousin, Kaiser Matanzima. K. D., as his fellow students called him, was in his third year at the university, and he was in line to become an important chief of one section of the Thembu tribe. Confident and outgoing, K. D. generously shared his allowance with Nelson, who had none.

Nelson admired his cousin greatly, and they became close friends. K. D. advised him to take up soccer, and since Nelson was taller and stronger than he had been three years earlier, he did better at the sport than he had at Clarkebury. He also listened seriously when K. D. urged him to study law.

Besides sports, Nelson took part in other student activities. In a drama production about Abraham Lincoln, he played the role of John Wilkes Booth, the Confederate loyalist who shot President Lincoln. The student who portrayed Lincoln, named Lincoln Mkentane, recited the Gettysburg Address, to a standing ovation from the audience.

Another student Nelson met at Fort Hare was Oliver Tambo, a quiet, thoughtful science student. Oliver had grown up in a family of poor peasants in Bizana, a village in Pondoland, in the northeast of the Transkei. His cheeks were marked with his tribe's ritual scarring. He was study-ing at Fort Hare on a scholarship.

The two did not become close friends at this time, because they lived in different housing—Nelson in the house for Methodist students, and Oliver in the Anglican house. However, they were both members of the Students' Christian Association (SCA). On Sundays students from the SCA walked into villages near Fort Hare to teach Bible classes. During the conversations on these walks, Nelson was impressed with Oliver, a serious student and a sharp, intelligent debater.

The food provided for students at Fort Hare was not much better than the food at Clarkebury or Healdtown. On weekends Nelson and his friends would walk into town for a satisfying restaurant meal. The restaurant was run by whites for white customers, but black customers were allowed to buy food at the kitchen door.

Outside black communities, Africans were faced with reminders like this that whites did not consider them equals. Like most black South Africans, Nelson tried not to make an issue of it. For instance, if a white person asked him to run an errand, he simply did it. Luckily, during his early life he was not often forced into contact with white people.

Nelson's social life blossomed at Fort Hare. Like his older cousin, K. D. Matanzima, he was tall and good-looking, with a winning smile. Ballroom dancing was a favorite student activity, and Nelson studied the steps and moves as seriously as he studied for his academic courses. He and his friends played phonograph records and practiced the fox-trot and the waltz in the dining hall, coached by another student.

One night, eager to try dancing with real women, they

sneaked out of their dormitory and walked to an African dance hall in a nearby village. Undergraduate students were not allowed at the dance hall, but Nelson, dressed in his suit, hoped to mingle with the crowd undetected. The young woman Nelson asked to dance with him turned out to be graceful as well as pretty. He couldn't help thinking how well he must look, whirling around the floor with her in his arms.

Unfortunately, Nelson discovered, that pretty young woman was Mrs. Bokwe, the wife of a noted scholar. Furthermore, her husband was the brother-in-law of Professor Matthews, who happened to be the head of student discipline at Fort Hare—and Dr. Matthews himself was watching Nelson from across the dance floor. Nelson was sure he was in serious trouble, and in the weeks afterward he studied his hardest. However, Dr. Matthews never called him in for breaking that rule.

Overall, Nelson didn't break many rules. He accepted the Methodist missionary regulations of his schools: no drinking, no smoking, no swearing. Although he never became particularly religious, he would keep to these ways of self-control for the rest of his life.

But every so often, Nelson and some of his fellow students at Fort Hare felt the need to let loose. Then they would steal out, under cover of night, to the university's farmland. They would help themselves to mealies, roast the ears of corn over an open fire, and sit around telling stories between mouthfuls. Enjoying themselves like country boys, Nelson and his friends could forget the pressures of becoming future leaders.

As Nelson studied and played, World War II broke out in Europe. Like most of his fellow students, Nelson was all for England and against Hitler's Germany. They gathered around the radio to listen to Prime Minister Winston Churchill's rousing speeches as London was being pounded by Nazi air raids.

In South Africa, however, a large section of the white population wanted South Africa to stay out of the war. Some even sided with Nazi Germany. The Afrikaners, of Dutch heritage, still longed for independence from Britain, and they were not eager to help their recent enemy fight Germany. To rally support for the war, former prime minister Jan Smuts toured South Africa and even visited Fort Hare to speak to the student body. Nelson and the other students applauded heartily as Smuts spoke of fighting to preserve freedom in Europe.

One member of the audience, however, was not impressed with Jan Smuts's speech. At a gathering afterward, a student named Nyathi Khongisa called Smuts a racist. The British offered education to black Africans, he said, but at the same time they refused to allow blacks equal rights. Although the British and the Dutch South Africans had their quarrels, Khongisa predicted that as whites, they would always unite to deny full freedom to blacks.

Nelson was shocked by these harsh words. Another student explained that Khongisa was a member of some black left-wing organization, called the African National Congress. Nelson didn't know much about the ANC, although Professor Matthews was a member. And one of Nelson's friends, Paul Mahabane, was the son of a man who had been president of the ANC.

Nelson invited Paul to spend a vacation with him at Mqhekezweni, and one day they went together into Umtata, the capital of the Transkei. As they stood outside the post office, a white man came by and asked Paul to go in and buy him some stamps. Nelson knew the man, a local magistrate, and he would have done the errand without thinking much about it. But Paul refused.

At first the white man was only annoyed that Paul

didn't obey him at once. But Paul made it clear that the white man had no right to expect obedience from a black man simply because he was black. At that, the white man became furious. "You'll pay dearly for this!" he threatened as he walked off.

Nelson was very uncomfortable as he watched the encounter. The magistrate knew that he was Jongintaba's ward, and maybe he would try to make *Nelson* pay dearly for the insult. On the other hand, Nelson admired his friend for standing up for himself. Here was more proof that a black person did not necessarily have to accept offensive treatment from white people.

The South African parliament did vote, by a small margin, to enter World War II on Britain's side, and Jan Smuts became prime minister again. The South African government urged blacks to join the war effort, but only as drivers, servants, and guards. Clearly, the white government didn't trust black South Africans with guns. In spite of this, 120,000 blacks volunteered to serve in the military, and half of all the South Africans killed in the war were black.

Meanwhile, Nelson was intent on his plans for his

future. Although he didn't say so to Regent Jongintaba, his goals had changed during his time at Fort Hare. He no longer wanted to become a tribal counselor to the next Thembu king, as the regent expected.

Like most of the students at Fort Hare, Nelson now planned to become a civil servant for the government of South Africa. A BA degree from Fort Hare would guarantee him a job as an interpreter in the Department of Native Affairs. And such a job would guarantee him a respected position in his community as well as a steady, comfortable income.

Nelson dreamed of supporting his mother, who had labored in poverty for as long as he could remember. When he became an interpreter for the civil service, he promised himself, he would give Nosekeni Fanny a house of her own. He would give her money to make life easier for her and his sisters.

During Nelson's second year at Fort Hare, he became involved in student politics. He ran for a position on the Student Representative Council, which was elected by the entire student body. Before the election, at a meeting for all students to discuss student affairs, two main complaints came up: The food was bad, and the Student

Representative Council had no real authority. The meeting voted to boycott the elections unless the principal, Dr. Kerr, agreed to improve the students' diet and to give the student council more powers.

Almost all the students boycotted the elections the next day, but twenty-five students did vote to elect Nelson and five others to the student council. Nelson and the other candidates, agreeing that the election was not valid, resigned from the council. However, under pressure from Dr. Kerr, the other five decided to accept positions on the council after all. Nelson was the only one who refused.

Dr. Kerr called Nelson into his office and asked him to think it over. If Nelson insisted on resigning from the council, he warned, he would be expelled from the school.

Nelson was torn—he felt responsible to all the students who had boycotted the elections. He had agreed that their demands were just. Was it right for him to abandon his fellow students in order to save himself?

On the other hand, he was shaken by the idea of being expelled before graduation, before receiving his BA degree. It would mean that he was throwing away his career, the good job with the Department of Native Affairs that he had dreamed about. He would not be able, after all, to take care of his mother the way he should—and the way she deserved. He would have to return to Mqhekezweni in disgrace.

Mulling these thoughts over that night, Nelson asked his friend and cousin Kaiser Matanzima for advice. K. D. counseled him not to give in to Dr. Kerr. When Nelson returned to Dr. Kerr's office the next morning, he was still not sure what he would say.

But in the moment of decision, Nelson heard himself declare that his conscience would not allow him to back down. The election had been fraudulent, and so the student body had not actually elected him to the council, and therefore it would not be right for him to serve. It was a matter of principle.

Even deeper than loyalty to his fellow students, Nelson refused to accept that Dr. Kerr had such power over his fate. Nelson felt that he had the right to resign from the council, and that it was unfair of the principal to give him such a harsh punishment for doing so. Maybe Nelson had the same stubborn streak as his father, who had defied the white magistrate and thereby lost his chieftainship and his wealth. Like Gadla Henry, Nelson

54

would not knuckle under to a power he did not respect.

Dr. Kerr was surprised. He was sure that he knew what was best for Nelson and the rest of the students, and he did not want to actually expel Nelson. And so he gave him another chance: At the end of the term in December, Nelson could go home and spend the vacation thinking his decision over again. If he decided to serve on the student council after all, he could return to Fort Hare, continue his education, and graduate with his BA.

Back in Mqhekezweni for vacation, Nelson had to tell Regent Jongintaba what he had done. The regent flew into a rage. He didn't see Nelson's resignation as a matter of principle at all. He thought Nelson was being stupid and childish, and also very ungrateful, after the regent had provided him with such an excellent education. He ordered Nelson to go back to Fort Hare, do as Dr. Kerr told him, and graduate as planned.

Nelson didn't argue with Regent Jongintaba. Maybe, at the end of the vacation, he would return to Fort Hare. Meanwhile, he was content to take up his life at Mqhekezweni and spend time with his foster brother, Justice, who had also left school.

At this point Nelson was twenty-two and Justice was

four years older, but the regent treated them both as children who had to be closely watched and managed. After a few weeks, Regent Jongintaba surprised Nelson and Justice with an announcement: He had arranged a marriage for each of them. Both of the young women were of good families, and both of the matches were suitable, in the parents' eyes.

However, Nelson and Justice were dismayed. Neither of them wanted to marry their intended brides. And Nelson knew for a fact that his intended bride would not want to marry him, because she was in love with Justice.

As far as Jongintaba was concerned, the matter was settled. By tribal law and custom, he had the right to arrange marriages for his children. He had already paid the bride-price for both young women, and the ceremonies would take place soon.

Nelson and Justice felt desperate. In their years away at school, they had absorbed Western ideas about romantic love, and they wanted to choose their own brides. Nelson went to his foster mother, Nkosikazi No-England, and persuaded her to argue with the regent on his behalf. But Jongintaba would not reconsider.

Privately, the young men discussed what to do. They

decided that the only way to escape the arranged marriages was to run away. And the logical place to run to was Johannesburg.

In making this decision, Nelson was throwing away a secure and prosperous future. He was also cutting his ties with Regent Jongintaba, his guardian and foster father. So far in his life, Nelson had not done much to live up to his original name, Rolihlahlah. But running away to Johannesburg would truly be "shaking the tree."

CHAPTER 5

CITY OF GOLD

IT WASN'T EASY FOR NELSON AND JUSTICE TO escape Regent Jongintaba's watchful eye. He knew they were discontented about the marriages he had arranged for them, and he was afraid they would get into trouble if he left them alone. Nelson still looked up to Justice, but Justice did not take his responsibilities seriously, and he brought out the reckless side of Nelson. Finally the regent had to leave Mqhekezweni for a whole week of tribal business in Umtata.

Nelson and Justice packed both their clothes into one suitcase. In the bottom of the suitcase Nelson tucked the old revolver that his father had left him. Nelson had heard many stories about gangsters and crime in the big city, and he wanted to be prepared.

The same morning that Jongintaba left, Nelson and

Justice took two of the regent's prize oxen to a cattle trader and sold them. They needed money for the long trip to Johannesburg, which was some three hundred miles to the north of Umtata. Their plan was to hire a car to take them to the local train station, where they would catch a train to Queenstown, at the border of the Transkei. From Queenstown they would take another train to Johannesburg. First, though, they would have to get travel documents in order to leave the Thembu tribal area.

Traveling across South Africa was difficult for blacks in 1941. By law they were required to carry a "Native pass," a document something like a passport. The pass showed where they lived, who the chief of their tribe was, and whether they had paid the poll tax. They could be punished with a fine or jail time if they couldn't produce a pass to show a policeman or official.

Nelson and Justice had valid passes, but since they intended to live and work someplace outside their reserve, they were also supposed to carry travel papers. These papers, in Nelson and Justice's case, should include a permit from their guardian—Jongintaba. However, the young men decided to deal with that problem when they reached the border of the Transkei.

But the first hitch in their plan cropped up as soon as Nelson and Justice arrived at the local railroad station. The station manager would not sell them tickets, because Regent Jongintaba had stopped by and told him not to. Nelson and Justice were shocked. The regent had anticipated their scheme, and he was one step ahead of them. But they had the hired car drive them to the next station, where they did succeed in catching a train.

In Queenstown, Nelson and Justice boldly went to the magistrate's office with a trumped-up story: They were on an errand for Regent Jongintaba. Since the regent was well known and respected in Queenstown, the magistrate was willing to make out the necessary travel papers for them. Unfortunately, he decided to call and notify the magistrate in Umtata first. Even more unfortunately, Regent Jongintaba happened to be sitting in the Umtata magistrate's office at that moment, and he took over the phone. "Arrest those boys!" he shouted.

Nelson, making good use of the law he had studied at Fort Hare, managed to talk the magistrate out of arresting them. Yes, he admitted, they had lied disgracefully, but they had not actually broken the law. The magistrate let the young men go with a warning.

But now Nelson and Justice were thoroughly humiliated. Worse, they were stuck in Queenstown without the travel papers they needed to take the train to Johannesburg. Luckily, Justice had a friend in the town, a fellow who worked for a white attorney.

Justice's friend said that the attorney's mother was about to drive to Johannesburg, and she might give them a ride. As it turned out, the white woman was willing to drive Nelson and Justice to the city—if they would pay her fifteen pounds. Fifteen pounds was a lot, almost all the money they had left. But it seemed to be their only choice, other than returning to Mqhekezweni in disgrace.

The next day they left Queenstown early in the morning, with the old woman driving and the young men in the backseat. Justice, always relaxed and friendly, began chatting with Nelson just as freely as if they were in Mqhekezweni. His cheerful, lively manner made the white woman fear that he was up to no good; she must have been used to black people who acted meek and quiet. She kept a suspicious eye on Justice throughout the long drive.

They traveled all day before crossing into the Transvaal,

the region on the high plateau that included both Johannes-burg and the capital of South Africa, Pretoria. Late at night, they neared Johannesburg. Nelson gaped at his first sight of the fabled City of Gold, grown rich by supplying the precious metal to the world. Electric lights glowed all over the city. A skyline of hulking buildings stood out darker than the dark sky.

It must be true, thought Nelson, all the stories he had heard about Johannesburg since he was a young boy. He stared at the cars streaming along the road—thousands more cars than he had seen in his entire life. If his dreams came true, he would have a car of his own.

They arrived at the white woman's daughter's home in a wealthy suburb, north of the city center. Nelson and Justice were allowed to stay here overnight—in the servants' quarters of the mansion. As Nelson went to sleep on the floor, he was excited and happy. In spite of the fact that he had no money, no job, and no place to live, he was sure that a wonderful future awaited him in Johannesburg.

At that time, Nelson did not realize how unlikely it was for any black African to find a wonderful future, or even a decent future, in this city. Although there certainly was wealth in Johannesburg, blacks were barred from the skilled, high-wage jobs that could earn them a fair share. The wealth in the gold mines came from black men working very hard, under miserable conditions, for low pay. As Chief Meligqili had declared at the celebration for Justice and Nelson, the black South Africans were slaves in their own country.

However, Justice and Nelson were young, brash, and optimistic. Their first morning in Johannesburg, they left the pleasant suburb, shielded from the noise and dust of the mines, and headed south across the ridge to Crown Mines. This was one of many mines on the Witwatersrand, the rocky range of hills with the world's largest deposits of gold ore.

The mine was quite a different place from the fairy-tale city Nelson had glimpsed the night before. It was a fenced-off moonscape of cratered bare dirt. Nelson expected that the offices of a gold mine, producing such fabulous wealth, would be stately buildings. But they were only tin-roofed shacks. Heavy machinery thudded and screeched, while white men shouted orders at black workers covered with dust.

As Nelson and Justice had been brought up with privileges in the Great Place, they assumed that they would receive special privileges at Crown Mines, also. In a way they were right, since Regent Jongintaba's name carried weight even here in Johannesburg. Because Nelson and his foster brother belonged to the regent's family, they did not have to take backbreaking jobs underground.

Justice was given an office job, and Nelson became a mine watchman. He felt important, dressed in a uniform and carrying a flashlight, a whistle, and a wooden club. His duty was to check the passes of all the black laborers as they entered and left the mine. The narrow route of the black miners from their compound to the mine was clearly marked with signs: BEWARE: NATIVES CROSSING HERE, as if they were dangerous animals.

These young black men from the reserves had signed contracts (which most of them could not read) committing them to at least nine months of laboring ten hours a day, six days a week, for less than a dollar per day. They worked deep underground, in sweltering heat. The stopes, or steplike excavations from which they dug the ore, were not high enough for a man to stand up straight.

In their little spare time, the black miners were encouraged to stay in their compounds, cut off from the rest of the city by a high brick wall. They were housed in barracks by tribe—Zulus with other Zulus, Xhosas with other Xhosas. The white authorities did not want the black Africans from various tribes to get to know one another and realize that they had a common enemy: the white boss.

The barracks housed twenty men to a room divided into concrete bunks. There was no privacy, unless a man hung a blanket in front of his bunk. The meals provided by the mine company consisted mainly of cornmeal mush. Worst of all, their families were not allowed to live with them or even visit. A miner was forced to go for almost a year at a time without seeing his wife or children.

Nelson could see what dreary lives these men led, working to exhaustion every day and housed like animals. But he and Justice were young and thoughtless. Instead of being sobered by the conditions of the black miners, they were proud of themselves. Instead of feeling guilty that they had lied and tricked their way to Johannesburg, they boasted to other workers about how clever they were.

Word got back to the headman of the miners, who

telegraphed Jongintaba. The regent return-telegraphed orders for his wards to be shipped back to Umtata immediately. Nelson and Justice tried to argue, and they even attempted to deceive their way back into their jobs at the mine, but the headman would not listen. "Get out of my sight!" he yelled. The young men had no choice but to leave, feeling humbler.

Nelson became even humbler when his suitcase was searched on his way out of the mine grounds. The watchman at the gate found the loaded revolver, Nelson's father's old gun, among the clothes. Possession of a gun by a black person was illegal in Johannesburg, and Nelson was lucky to get away without jail time and with paying only a small fine.

In spite of the regent's orders, Justice and Nelson were still determined not to return home. But now they were out on the street, without jobs or a place to live. Fortunately, Justice had friends he could stay with in the city. And Nelson, although he was far from his tribal grounds, could still count on support from his kinfolk.

Nelson looked up a cousin, Garlick Mbekeni, who lived in a township near the mines. Mbekeni rented one of the "matchbox" houses, so called because they were the shape of a matchbox and very small, that the city provided for black workers. He made his living by hawking clothing on the streets.

Friendly and helpful, Mbekeni welcomed Nelson. He gave him a place to sleep, and he encouraged him to talk about what he would do next. Nelson explained that his real ambition was to become a lawyer.

That was a very high goal for a black South African, but not impossible. World War II was still going on, and this had created a window of opportunity for a few ambitious black men. Businesses were booming as they produced supplies for the army, and they needed more skilled workers. At the same time, many white South African workers were off fighting. Therefore, employers were more willing to hire blacks, and some of the laws restricting black South Africans were relaxed.

Mbekeni approved of Nelson's ambition, and he asked around about who might be able to help his cousin. He decided that Walter Sisulu—"one of our best people in Johannesburg," Mbekeni told Nelson—was the right man. Sisulu was a real estate agent, not a lawyer, but he dealt with lawyers all the time. Sisulu was a sharp businessman, he had many connections, and he was known for helping other people, especially people from his native Transkei.

Walter Sisulu was indeed the right man. He would become one of the most important influences on Nelson Mandela's life.

CHAPTER 6
INDEPENDENCE

AT SISULU'S OFFICE IN DOWNTOWN JOHANNESBURG, Mandela's cousin Mbekeni introduced them. Sisulu was a short man in his late twenties, only six years older than Mandela. He wore glasses, and he had light skin and a kindly, gap-toothed smile. Mandela was impressed that Sisulu seemed so comfortable with city ways and that he spoke English so fluently, better than Mandela. Mandela thought the other man must be a college graduate, but later he learned that Sisulu had dropped out of school when he was sixteen.

Unlike Nelson Mandela, Walter Sisulu had had a difficult upbringing. His white father had never acknowledged him, and Walter had grown up in a poor village in the Engcobo district, in the western part of the Transkei. His family tried to bring him up to be submissive toward whites, as was expected, but Walter scorned that behavior.

At age sixteen, Sisulu left home to come to Johannesburg and work in the mines. Hating the mines, he soon went on to a series of factory jobs. He hated those jobs too, and he especially hated his white bosses. He did not accept the injustices that blacks in Johannesburg suffered all the time from whites. Once he had even been sentenced to a short prison term for defending a black passenger from a white ticket collector.

Highly motivated to become his own boss and help other black people, Walter Sisulu saw an opportunity in real estate. Although blacks were not allowed to own property in much of Johannesburg, there were still some areas of the city, including Alexandra and Sophiatown, where they had owned small parcels of land for generations. Sisulu set up a real estate agency to serve black sellers and buyers, and he became a success in business and a leader in his community.

The day of their meeting in 1941, Sisulu was struck with Mandela's ambition and dignity. The tall, handsome young man facing him might be naive about life in a big city, but he carried himself like a born leader. As an independent-thinking black man, Sisulu liked the fact that

Mandela had left Fort Hare rather than knuckle under to the white principal. He approved of Mandela's goals to finish his degree by correspondence course and to become a lawyer.

Leaning back in his chair, Sisulu chewed his lip and thought for a moment. He often did business with a young white attorney named Lazar Sidelsky. Sidelsky was interested in the education of black South Africans, and he donated money to black schools. Sisulu said he would talk to Sidelsky and see if he would hire Mandela as a law clerk.

On Sisulu's recommendation, Sidelsky was willing to give Mandela a job in his law office and train him. He even waived the usual initial fee that an attorney charged a clerk. It was extremely unusual in Johannesburg for a white attorney to hire a black clerk, but Sidelsky sympathized with the plight of black Africans. He was convinced that they could better themselves and help their people if only they could receive proper education.

And like Sisulu, Sidelsky was impressed with Mandela's courtesy and confidence at their first meeting. They agreed that he could complete his BA degree by correspondence while he was serving his legal apprenticeship working for

Sidelsky. Then Mandela would study law at the University of Witwatersrand.

Although Lazar Sidelsky respected Walter Sisulu as a businessman, he did not approve of his involvement in politics. Sisulu was active in the African National Congress. Sidelsky thought he was a troublemaker, and he warned Mandela to keep away from him. He told Mandela he could do more for his people through proving "that there's one black attorney who's honest and successful" than by protesting for black rights.

Sidelsky also warned Mandela against an employee in his office: Gaur Radebe, another black clerk. But Mandela admired Radebe, who was ten years older and coolly unconcerned about telling whites his political views. He was fluent in Zulu, Sotho, and English; he was a member of the ANC and also belonged to the South African Communist Party. Radebe was organizing the African Mine Workers Union, to improve the miserable conditions of the black miners on the Witwatersrand.

Radebe showed his troublemaking side on Mandela's first day at Sidelsky's firm, at the morning tea break. Although most whites in Johannesburg wouldn't think of taking tea with blacks, the secretaries wanted to show

how open-minded they were: They would offer Mandela and Radebe tea from the same tray as their own cups. However, beforehand one of the secretaries explained to Mandela, in the nicest way, that they had bought two new cups especially for the two black clerks. Mandela understood her unspoken message: The white secretaries were not quite open-minded enough to drink from the same cups as black people.

Gaur Radebe knew quite well that he and Mandela were expected to take the two new cups, but he mischievously took one of the old ones instead. They all watched to see what Mandela would do. Torn between offending the secretaries and losing the respect of his office mate, Mandela pretended that he didn't want any tea. From then on, he took his tea by himself in the kitchen.

This was only the beginning of the uneasy balance Nelson had to maintain while working closely with white people. Another time, when one of the secretaries was taking dictation from Mandela, a white customer came into the office. The secretary, embarrassed to be seen doing work for a black man, pretended that she was sending Mandela on an errand. She handed him a sixpence and asked him to go to the drugstore and buy shampoo for her.

Mandela did not want to make a scene, so he went out and bought the shampoo.

Outside Sidelsky's office, the racism was more straightforward. The post offices had separate entrances for whites and blacks, and separate counters inside. In many public parks, blacks were not allowed; if they were, the benches were marked EUROPEANS ONLY. Public toilets were always segregated, and if there was only one toilet, it was for whites.

Likewise, there were two sets of elevators in the larger buildings of the city. One was marked EUROPEANS, and the other NON EUROPEANS & GOODS. In other words, blacks were only allowed to use the freight elevator.

However, Mandela's employer, Lazar Sidelsky, did not go along with this racist mind-set. "He was the first white man who treated me as a human being," Mandela wrote later. Sidelsky, for his part, was happy with Mandela, who was disciplined, organized, and trustworthy. "It was a pleasure to have him around," he remembered years later. "He had an intelligent grasp of what was required."

Besides giving Mandela the practical experience he needed to qualify for the law profession, Sidelsky was careful to explain the legal purpose of each job he gave

Mandela to do. He lent Mandela fifty pounds, a large sum of money, to get started in the city. He even gave him an old suit, so that Mandela could be properly dressed for the office.

Another man in the office who ignored the racist customs was Mandela's white office mate, Nat Bregman. He was also a clerk serving his legal apprenticeship. Bregman was bright and thoughtful, and the two hit it off right away.

Bregman, like Gaur Radebe, was a member of the South African Communist Party. He urged Mandela to think about joining the party himself. Mandela accompanied Bregman to lectures and meetings, but he wasn't sure about joining. He didn't like the party's bias against religion, and he didn't think they understood the main problem in South Africa: racial injustice.

However, Mandela was delighted to be invited to parties with the people Bregman knew. The first time he went to one of these parties, he was amazed to find a thoroughly mixed-race social gathering. This was almost unheard of in South Africa.

There were whites, blacks, Indians, and Coloureds (as South Africans called mixed-race people), and they all mingled without any regard to skin color or ethnic origin.

Mandela was almost as surprised to meet a man—a man with an MA degree, at that!—who was not even wearing a tie. Mandela was always determined to be well dressed, and he had agonized over whether he had the right clothes for the party.

Although Mandela now had a steady job, he still had to find a place to live. In 1941 the black population of Johannesburg was more than 250,000, and every week hundreds more black South Africans arrived in the city to look for work. The whites of Dutch heritage, the Afrikaners, were alarmed at the "black peril," as they termed the growth of the black population. The city government restricted the blacks to living in "locations," or townships, apart from white residences.

These places where blacks were allowed to live, such as the township of Alexandra, were already overcrowded. First Mandela boarded at the home of Reverend Mabutho, a fellow Thembu. But after only a few days, Mabutho discovered how Mandela had tricked and run away from his guardian, Regent Jongintaba, and he asked him to leave.

Next Mandela rented a room from a neighbor of

Mabutho's. The neighbor, Mr. Xhoma, owned his house, which was unusual with all the restrictions the white authorities placed on where blacks could own property. Mandela's room was only a tin-roofed shack with a dirt floor, but he was glad to have it. He was also grateful that the Xhomas always invited him to Sunday lunch, which was his only hot meal of the week.

Nelson Mandela's new home, Alexandra, was a slum. There was no indoor plumbing, and several overcrowded houses shared each water tap. Half-dressed, skinny children and stray dogs roamed the dirt streets. There was no electricity and no streetlights.

With the poverty, many young men were attracted to street gangs, and crime was a serious problem. The police made regular raids into Alexandra, but mainly to harass the *shebeens*, or saloons, that illegally served home-brewed beer. The police also concentrated on arresting people who could not produce their passes. (Across South Africa, 350,000 people were arrested every year for pass violations.) Gangsters controlled the streets at night, and in the morning it was not unusual to see a corpse with bullet holes or knife wounds lying in the gutter.

Still, Mandela found Alexandra an exciting place to live. Tribes from all over South Africa mixed freely in Alexandra, and people helped one another not because they belonged to the same tribe, but because they were neighbors and shared the same difficulties. During his years at Clarkebury, Healdtown, and Fort Hare, Mandela had gradually developed a sense of belonging to a wider community than the Thembu tribe. In Johannesburg he finally came to think of himself as a South African.

It was also clearer to him that the white government encouraged separation of the tribes in order to control black Africans. The blacks far outnumbered the whites in South Africa, and the whites feared that the blacks would join forces. United, the blacks might "dump all of you into the sea," as Mandela's office mate Gaur Radebe impudently threatened their boss, Lazar Sidelsky. But as long as the Xhosa tribes thought of the Zulus as enemies, and the Thembus refused to associate with the Swazis, and the tribes could not even understand one another's languages, the whites could keep the upper hand.

Nelson Mandela had certainly lived in poverty as a child in Qunu, but now he felt much poorer in Johannesburg. He was lucky to be working as a law clerk, but his salary was only two pounds a week. Out of that he had to pay for rent, food, bus fare to work, correspondence course fees, and candles for light by which to study at night. Mandela ate bread more than anything else, and sometimes he walked the twelve-mile round trip to work and back in order to save the four-pence bus fare.

In spite of having to scrape by this way, Mandela was happy to be independent for the first time in his life. Ever since he had arrived in Mqhekezweni at the age of twelve, he had been known as the ward of Regent Jongintaba. His food and clothing, his schooling, and his place in the community had all been given to him by the regent. Mandela had enjoyed the privileges of his position, but now he was proud to find that he could take care of himself.

Mandela was busy, working at Sidelsky's law firm during the day and studying at night. Still, he found time to strike up friendships with young women. One of them was Ellen Nkabinde, a teacher in Alexandra. Mandela had known her a little at Healdtown, and now they became good friends. Since neither of them had much time or money, their dates consisted mostly of walks in the nearby hills.

Mandela's friendship with Ellen showed how far he had come. Growing up, he had been taught that he could be close only to other members of the Thembu tribe, or at least to Africans who spoke the Xhosa language. Ellen was a Swazi, from a tribe in eastern South Africa. Some of Mandela's friends, still trapped in tribal attitudes, advised him not to associate with her. But he paid no attention.

Mandela also developed a crush on his landlord's prettiest daughter, Didi Xhoma, who worked as a white family's servant in a suburb of Johannesburg. Mandela was so smitten that he longed to propose marriage to Didi, but she paid him no attention. She already had a boyfriend, probably a gangster, who wore expensive suits and drove Didi around in a car.

One day, as Mandela was returning to Alexandra on a bus, he sat down next to another young man. Judging by his new, ultrastylish clothes, it was likely that he was a gangster. Mandela himself loved nice clothes as much as ever, but he was forced to make do every day with one secondhand suit and with wearing the same shirt several days in a row. To his humiliation, he noticed the other man moving carefully aside so that his well-tailored jacket would not touch Mandela's shabby old suit.

Meanwhile, Regent Jongintaba had given up trying to control his former ward's destiny. At the end of 1941 they met again in Johannesburg. Jongintaba did not reproach Mandela for running away. He seemed to accept the fact that Mandela was an independent adult on his own path. He asked with fatherly concern about Mandela's life in the city and his plans for himself.

The regent was old now, and not in good health. Only six months later, Mandela received word of his death. Traveling to Mqhekezweni with Justice to pay his respects, Mandela felt guilty. If it were not for Jongintaba, Mandela would still be scratching out a bare living in Qunu, or perhaps working himself to death underground in a gold mine. He felt he had not been grateful enough.

During the visit to his former home in the Transkei, Mandela realized how far he had traveled from his tribal background. Old friends even told him that he now spoke Xhosa with a Zulu accent. He struggled with the feeling that he was letting down his father, who had sent him to the regent to be groomed as a tribal counselor. And didn't Mandela owe it to Regent Jongintaba, his second father, to fulfill his traditional role? After all, Justice had decided to remain in the Transkei and take over his father's position as the new ruler of the Thembu.

But Mandela had come too far to fit back into his old life. Even before the ceremony to install Justice as the new chief, he returned to Johannesburg.

CHAPTER 7
POLITICS

AT THE END OF 1942, NELSON MANDELA AT LAST passed his examinations for a BA degree. He traveled to Fort Hare for the graduation ceremony, wearing a new suit bought with money borrowed from Walter Sisulu. In the audience were the two women who had mothered him, Nosekeni Fanny and Regent Jongintaba's widow, No-England. Mandela's cousin Kaiser Matanzima was also there. Matanzima seemed set on his own course in life, which was to become the chief of a section of the Thembu, in the western Transkei.

After the graduation ceremonies, Matanzima tried to talk Mandela into returning to the Transkei. He approved of Mandela's goal to become an attorney—after all, he was the one who had urged his cousin at Fort Hare to study law. But Matanzima felt that once Mandela had qualified as an attorney, he should come back and offer the Thembu tribe his valuable leadership.

However, Mandela was clearer than ever that he wanted to serve all the people of South Africa, not only one tribe. He would become a lawyer, but then he intended to use his law degree as an entry into South African politics.

Back in Johannesburg, Mandela moved from Alexandra to Orlando, a township even farther out of the city. Orlando had been created by the city of Johannesburg especially for "the better class of native." The idea was not only to keep the blacks who worked in Johannesburg away from the white suburbs, but also to control them. A superintendent decided which people deserved to rent the houses in Orlando, and the gate of the fenced township was guarded by a policeman checking permits.

The design of the suburb, straight rows of small houses exactly alike on small plots along rutted dirt streets, was dreary. The cramped houses had cement floors and tin roofs without ceilings. The whole development was overshadowed by a huge power station. It was a safer and more sanitary community than Alexandra, but not as friendly or exciting.

84

However, Walter Sisulu lived in Orlando with his mother, Ma Sisulu. Mandela had ignored Sidelsky's advice and become good friends with the real estate agent. The Sisulus' small brick house near the railway line always seemed to be full of people, and there was always a political discussion going on. Mandela spent much of his free time there.

One of the regular visitors at the Sisulus' was a friend of Mandela's from Fort Hare, Oliver Tambo. He had the same quiet manner Mandela remembered, and the same keen intelligence. Oliver had been doing graduate work at Fort Hare, but he was expelled for leading a student protest.

Walter Sisulu was an active member of the African National Congress, and his home served as a kind of recruiting center for new members. For many years the ANC had done almost nothing, but in 1940 a new president, Alfred Xuma, began to revive the organization. Dr. Xuma increased the ANC membership, built up the treasury, and encouraged members to let go of the tribal divisions among them. However, the ANC remained a middle-class movement, with not much appeal for black miners or farmers.

In spite of Lazar Sidelsky's advice to stay away from politics, Mandela was attracted to the ANC. He approved of their policy to welcome members of every tribe, resisting the white government's strategy of keeping the blacks separated. The government's racist policies harmed all the black people of South Africa, no matter which tribe they came from.

Early in the 1940s, the members of the ANC felt that there might be international support for them. In 1941 both US president Franklin Roosevelt and British prime minister Winston Churchill signed the Atlantic Charter. This document declared "the rights of all peoples to choose the form of government under which they will live."

Roosevelt and Churchill intended the Atlantic Charter as a manifesto against Nazi Germany's aggression. They did not mean to criticize the European nations (including Great Britain) who had seized territory in Africa. Still, the charter inspired liberation movements in many African states. And to Mandela, Sisulu, and others in the ANC, it led to an obvious conclusion: If the people of European countries deserved to choose their own government, so did African people.

Nelson Mandela began his law studies at the University of Witwatersrand, just north of Johannesburg, in 1943. He was the only black student in the law school. At that time a few black students were allowed to attend classes at the university, although they could not use the campus sports facilities or the swimming pool.

Most of Mandela's fellow students barely tolerated him. In lecture halls, if he sat down next to a white student, the other student would move. The white law professor, Mr. Hahlo, stated openly that neither blacks nor women were capable of mastering the difficult discipline of the law. Unfortunately, Nelson Mandela did not prove Professor Hahlo wrong, at least through his academic achievement. Between work at the law firm and his growing political involvement, Mandela neglected his studies.

However, a number of the white students were not racist, and Mandela made some important friends among them. Later they remembered him from law school days as quiet and dignified, reserved but friendly. It must have been hard for Mandela to relax, at least in public, with them. One time in a café, his white friends were refused service because a *kaffir* (an insulting term for blacks) was with them.

Two of these white friends were Ruth First and Joe Slovo, who would later marry. They were both from immigrant Jewish families, and they were deeply involved in the South African Communist Party. Another friend, George Bizos, was the son of Greek immigrants.

Bram Fischer, a part-time lecturer at the law school, was the most surprising member of this group, since he came from a leading Afrikaner family. As Mandela noted later, Fischer could have become prime minister of South Africa. Instead he chose to work for freedom and justice for all South Africans.

For the first time, Mandela also became good friends with some of the Indian students, including Ismail Meer and J. N. Singh. Singh was a member of the South African Communist Party, and Meer was a leader in the Transvaal Indian Congress, which worked to protect the rights of the Indian community. Meer's apartment in downtown Johannesburg served as a student gathering center, and Mandela sometimes slept there after late-night parties.

One day when Mandela was with his Indian friends, they all boarded a tram together. Indians were legally allowed on trams, but blacks were not. The tram conductor called Mandela a *kaffir* and ordered him to get off.

When Meer and Singh argued with the conductor, the whole group was arrested.

The next day in court, Bram Fischer appeared as the attorney to defend Mandela, Meer, and Singh. The judge seemed to be intimidated, because Fischer's grandfather and father were well-known Afrikaners with considerable political influence. The charges were dropped, but Mandela noted that the judge was letting them go only because Bram Fischer was on their side.

Little by little, Nelson found himself drawn deeper into the political struggle going on in South Africa. On the one hand, there were the people in power: the mine owners, the white government, and all the whites who were afraid of losing their special status. The powerful even included some black leaders who kept their own status by cooperating with the whites. On the other hand, there were the vast majority of South Africans who had no representation in the government: the blacks, the Coloureds, the Asians. These people had only a few choices. They could go along with the unjust system, they could protest peacefully, or they could rebel by force.

One of the many ways the system affected the lives of black South Africans was through the bus monopoly in Alexandra. The bus company seemed to have a secure hold on the black workers in Alexandra, because their jobs were in Johannesburg, but black people were not allowed to live there. The "Native" bus was their only means of transportation from the township into the city, six miles away. There were no trains or trams from Alexandra, and cars were an unheard-of luxury. The bus was crowded, its stops were inconvenient, and it was often late—but it was the only choice besides walking the twelve-mile round trip.

In August of 1943, the bus company announced that bus fare would increase from four pence to five. The people of Alexandra, who could barely afford four pence, were angry. Gaur Radebe, Mandela's former office mate, seized the chance to organize a bus boycott. Rather than pay more for the same poor service, the people would stop taking the bus.

For nine days the buses ran almost empty, as twenty thousand commuters marched to work along the bus route. They had to get up at three a.m. and they didn't return home until nine p.m., but it was worth it for the satisfaction of withholding their money from the bus company. It was also satisfying to the boycotters that the thousands of people walking on the roads tied up traffic for miles.

Mandela marched with the boycotters, and he was inspired by participating in this mass movement. For once, the black workers enjoyed a certain amount of power. The boycott was successful, and the bus company reset the fare to four pence.

Around the time of the boycott Mandela met Anton Lembede, one of a very few black lawyers in South Africa. Lembede, a Zulu, believed passionately that black South Africans of all tribes must unite against white oppression. He wanted to launch a young, more active section of the African National Congress. He believed they needed to include working-class people as well as teachers, government employees, and other black professionals.

To get approval for these plans, a group of young ANC members, including Nelson Mandela, went to see Alfred Xuma, the president. Walter Sisulu, Anton Lembede, and Oliver Tambo were also part of the group. Dr. Xuma had a large house and a clinic in Sophiatown, a multiracial community on the west side of Johannesburg.

The young men hoped to persuade Dr. Xuma that a Youth League was the way to turn the ANC into an organization with mass support. They believed that if enough people joined, they could make real change happen in South Africa. The group had already drawn up a declaration of principles for the Youth League. And they had outlined a campaign to recruit Africans from all walks of life, not only the middle class.

But Dr. Xuma firmly believed that the way to work with white people was very politely, as if both sides were English gentlemen. Writing letters and forming delegations were courteous ways to protest injustice; strikes and boycotts were not. Besides, he told the young men in a fatherly way, black Africans were too disorganized and undisciplined to make mass action work.

The Youth League planners did not agree. Seeing that Dr. Xuma would not support them, they decided to go ahead without him. And in spite of Dr. Xuma's opposition, in December 1943 the national meeting of the ANC in Bloemfontein approved the formation of a Youth League. On Easter Sunday, 1944, at the Bantu Men's Social Center in downtown Johannesburg, the Youth League was officially launched. Anton Lembede, Oliver Tambo, and Walter Sisulu were elected officers, while Nelson Mandela was elected to the executive committee. In a manifesto or public declaration, the Youth

League stated bluntly that black South Africans must join forces to overthrow white supremacy and establish a truly democratic government.

The Youth League's manifesto reviewed the history of the laws the white government had enacted against black South Africans in the last forty years: The 1913 Natives Land Act had taken 87 percent of the country, including the most valuable farmland and the mines, away from blacks. The Urban Areas Act of 1923 had created fenced-off sections for blacks near cities, segregated from white residents. The Color Bar Act of 1926 made it illegal for Africans to pursue skilled trades, reserving those better jobs for whites. The Native Administration Act of 1927 had made the white government, rather than the tribal chiefs, the real rulers even within the native reserves. Up until 1936, a limited number of blacks had been able to vote in the Cape Province, but the Representation of Natives Act took even that small bit of political influence away.

Whites often justified these laws by explaining that black South Africans were not ready to govern themselves, and that whites knew best how to run the country for the benefit of the "natives." The ANC Youth League rejected this explanation. "We believe that the national liberation of Africans will be achieved by Africans themselves," they declared. These were stirring words, and Nelson Mandela believed them wholeheartedly. But at that point he felt uneasy about getting completely involved in the ANC. He was working full-time and trying to study in his few spare hours. And he was about to further complicate his life with family commitments.

CHAPTER 8

FAMILY MAN AND POLITICAL MAN

EVELYN MASE WAS A PRETTY TWENTY-TWO-
year-old woman from the Transkei. In 1944 she was living with her older brother, Sam, in Orlando East. Both
of their parents were dead, and Evelyn had come to
Johannesburg to attend high school. They were distant
cousins of Walter Sisulu's, and at first they had lived with
the Sisulus.

Evelyn was training to be a nurse at the Johannesburg Non-European General Hospital. She had become
good friends with Walter's future wife, Albertina, who
was also training for a nursing career. Evelyn often visited
Ma Sisulu, Walter's mother, who treated her like a daughter. All the Sisulus thought highly of Evelyn.

One day Ma Sisulu introduced Evelyn to Nelson
Mandela. As Evelyn told it later, "He was handsome and

charming and he made me laugh." Mandela quickly fell in love with her, and she with him.

A few months later Nelson and Evelyn were married at the Native Commissioner's Court in Johannesburg. Walter Sisulu and his wife, Albertina, who had gotten married a short time earlier, were their witnesses. The simple ceremony was the extent of the wedding, since Nelson and Evelyn could not afford to hold a wedding reception.

At Walter and Albertina's wedding reception, Dr. Xuma had given a speech in which he warned Albertina, "You are marrying a man who is already married. He is married to the nation." Someone could have said the same thing to Evelyn, who had no idea that her husband was going to devote his life to South African politics. She knew he was interested in politics, but she thought he would outgrow it. She expected him to become a successful lawyer and family man, and she hoped that they would move back to the Transkei.

Housing was a problem for the Mandelas, as it always was for black people in the cities of South Africa. First they lived with Evelyn's brother in Orlando East. Then they moved in with Evelyn's sister and her husband, who worked as a clerk at City Deep Mines.

At the beginning of 1946 they became eligible to rent a two-room house in Orlando East and finally a three-room house in Orlando West. These houses were in great demand, and the reason the Mandelas qualified was that they had a child. A son had been born in 1945. They named their baby Madiba Thembekile, and they called him Thembi.

Like all the thousands of houses in Orlando, the Mandelas' had a tin roof, a cement floor, and a bucket toilet. There were streetlights along the dusty dirt roads, but no electricity in the houses. Still, the Mandelas were proud and happy to have their own home. Evelyn, a homebody, delighted in keeping house, cooking, gardening on their small plot of land, and taking care of her family.

Nelson was overjoyed with his son. According to Thembu tradition, he was doing his duty to carry on his clan name, Madiba, as well as the Mandela line. Besides, he loved taking care of Thembi: feeding him, bathing him, and tucking him in bed with a story at night.

Mandela's life followed a disciplined pattern that suited him very well. He rose early every morning, went jogging, ate a light breakfast, and left for the office. He stayed up late, studying or at meetings, but he didn't need much sleep.

Now that the Mandelas had a home of their own, although it was small, they welcomed family members or friends who needed a place to stay. If there were many visitors, the Mandelas made up beds on the floor and somehow squeezed everyone in. Nelson's cousin Kaiser Matanzima was a frequent guest, and he hadn't given up trying to persuade Mandela to move back to the Transkei.

Mandela's sister Leabie came from the Transkei to live with him. She studied at Orlando High School, as Evelyn had done a few years before, and she also helped Evelyn around the house. Leabie noticed that Evelyn, although she tolerated Nelson's political activities, was not very interested in politics herself.

Meanwhile, the African Mine Workers Union (AMWU), organized by Gaur Radebe and others in the early 1940s, had been asking the mine owners for better pay. Black miners were paid less than one-tenth as much as white miners, and there had been a drought in 1945, raising the price of food. The AMWU also asked for housing where the miners' families could live with them, instead of single-sex barracks. And they wanted paid leave and better food. But the Chamber of Mines, the organization of the mine owners, ignored these requests.

In August of 1946, seventy thousand union workers went out on strike—they stopped working. Eight gold mines on the Witwatersrand came to a sudden halt, and so did the wealth pouring out of the mines into the white mine-owners' pockets. The mining companies, backed by Prime Minister Smuts's government, did not even consider negotiating with the miners. They ordered troops to charge at the strikers with bayonets. Twelve black miners were killed, more than twelve hundred were wounded, and the fifty leaders of the strike were arrested.

The Natives Representative Council, including Professor Matthews from Fort Hare, as well as Dr. James Moroka and the Zulu chief Albert Luthuli, happened to be meeting at the time of the strike. They were outraged that the government ignored the council as well as the miners' union. It was finally clear that the Natives Representative Council, supposedly meant to communicate the blacks' concerns to the white government, was useless. One council member called it a "toy telephone."

Dr. Xuma, the cautious president of the ANC, criticized the communists in the miners' union for taking such a rash action. But Mandela and the Youth League of the ANC saw it differently. Mandela had many relatives

99

working in the mines, and he respected the strike leaders, including J. B. Marks, the president of the AMWU. He admired the organization and determination of the miners and of their courageous leaders.

After the strike had been put down, the Chamber of Mines issued the absurd statement that trade unionism was "still beyond the understanding of the tribal Native." A union, they said, would be "detrimental to the ordinary mine Native in his present stage of development." The troops' bayonets had certainly been "detrimental," and the AMWU was destroyed. That same year, the gold mines of South Africa sold 102 million pounds' worth of gold.

Since World War II ended in 1945, there had been a growing fear of communism in South Africa, as in the United States. Now that Nazi Germany and its allies had been defeated, the new enemy seemed to be a worldwide communist conspiracy, the "red menace," led by the Soviet Union. Many whites saw labor unions as fronts for communists. They were also afraid that blacks would be attracted to the Communist Party as a way to overthrow white domination.

Mandela knew several members of the South African Communist Party personally, and many of them, such as

J. B. Marks, were also members of the ANC. He respected their commitment to oppressed workers around the world, and he was impressed that they welcomed people of all races. However, he still had mixed feelings about the Communist Party. He thought that in South Africa, the problem was not so much the upper class taking advantage of workers as it was the oppression of blacks by whites. He was afraid that the white communists would try to use the ANC for their own purposes.

Some in the ANC had hoped that Prime Minister Jan Smuts would support their cause, but there was an election coming up. Smuts needed to win political support from the Afrikaners, the South Africans of Dutch heritage, who were more numerous than other whites. Black South Africans, on the other hand, could not vote in national elections.

Most Afrikaners believed fervently that whites were superior to all other races, and they quoted passages from the Bible that seemed to support this idea. They felt threatened that the black population of South Africa was growing so much faster than the white population, especially in the cities. They were also worried about the increasing number of "foreigners," as they called South Africans of Indian origin, in the urban areas.

The National Party, led by Daniel Malan, attracted many Afrikaners. The National Party's main idea was expressed in the term "apartheid," Afrikaans for "apartness." It meant keeping blacks away from whites, to preserve what Afrikaners thought of as the purity of the white race, and to keep blacks in an inferior position. As for Indians, the National Party wanted them out of the country.

The same year as the gold miners' strike, the Smuts government tried to please the Afrikaners by passing the Asiatic Land Tenure and Indian Representation Act, also known (more frankly) as the Ghetto Act. This act placed strict controls on the Indians of South Africa: Indians could only live, do business, or own property in certain limited areas.

The Indian community refused to accept such outrageous treatment. In response, they conducted a campaign to protest the law. The protests, including mass rallies and occupation of whites-only areas, went on for two years. Two thousand Indians, among them Mandela's friends Ismail Meer and J. N. Singh, went to prison for deliberately violating Ghetto Act laws. The ANC sympathized with the Indians, and Mandela admired their well-organized protests.

During this period, Mandela drew closer to his Indian friends. He went to friendly gatherings in downtown Johannesburg, where Indians, progressive whites, and blacks would share curry dinners and talk politics. Ismail Meer and Ruth First were both regulars at these events.

Mandela recognized a similarity between South Africa and India, another country colonized by Europeans where the natives were struggling for their rights. He admired the work of Mahatma Gandhi, the brave and disciplined leader of the Indian movement for independence from Britain. Gandhi's tactic of nonviolent disobedience, practiced over many years, finally forced the British Empire to let India go. In August of 1947, India became an independent nation.

At the beginning of 1947, Nelson Mandela decided to leave Lazar Sidelsky's law firm in order to study law full-time. This was a risky step, because it would make his family dependent on Evelyn's salary as a nurse. But Mandela felt that a law degree was the credential he needed in order to become a political leader, and studying in his spare time was too slow and difficult.

A few months later Evelyn was pregnant again and had

to go on unpaid maternity leave. Nelson took out loans from the Bantu Welfare Trust at the South African Institute of Race Relations, but they still had a hard time paying the bills. When the baby was born, she turned out to be sickly, and she needed extra care. The doctors couldn't say what was wrong with Makaziwe, as she was named. At the age of nine months, the baby died, and Evelyn and Nelson were grief-stricken.

Meanwhile, in July, Anton Lembede, the fiery president of the ANC Youth League, suddenly fell ill during a meeting. Mandela and the others took him to the hospital, but he died that night. He was only thirty-three years old. However, Peter Mda, who took over the presidency of the Youth League, proved to be an effective leader. Mandela became secretary of the Youth League, and he began the work of setting up branches in different parts of the country. One of the most successful branches was at his former university, Fort Hare.

Early in 1948 the news came from India that Mahatma Gandhi, the role model for passive resistance in South Africa and around the globe, had been assassinated. It was a sad reminder that a hero, even a successful one, might have to suffer great sacrifices.

As secretary of the Youth League, Nelson Mandela spent a great deal of time traveling to recruit new members for the ANC. During one of these trips in 1948, he spent three months in Cape Town, on the southwest coast of South Africa. It was his first trip to Cape Town, and while he was there he rode the cable car up Table Mountain. Up on the flat-topped peak overlooking Cape Town, he gazed west toward Robben Island. That was the small piece of land where, long ago, the British had imprisoned the Xhosa leader Makana.

Nelson Mandela was now completely absorbed in his work for the ANC. When he was home, he attended political meetings every night and every weekend. His law studies suffered. He did not pay much attention to the politics of white South Africa, although an important election was coming up in May. The National Party, under Daniel Malan, was challenging Prime Minister Jan Smuts and his United Party.

The National Party, representing the Afrikaners, believed that South Africa rightfully belonged to them, not the British whites. They still hated the British for conquering the Cape and other parts of South Africa colonized by Dutch settlers. They were still angry at Jan Smuts and the United Party for leading South Africa into World War II, which they called "England's war" with Germany. The National Party thought the Nazis had some good ideas—including white supremacy.

In the campaign of 1948, Daniel Malan stressed his belief in apartheid. As Mandela commented, it was a new term for an old idea. "Apartheid" meant that whites and people of color, especially black Africans, should not mix. They should live in separate places, attend separate schools, and use separate public facilities such as toilets and drinking fountains.

This was more or less the way the South African government had run things from the beginning. And Prime Minister Smuts, the leader of the United Party, also believed that whites were superior to blacks. He had crushed the black miners' strike and approved the unjust Ghetto Act. He had done nothing to change the many laws, as well as informal customs, keeping the races separate and favoring whites over everyone else.

But even Smuts called apartheid "a crazy concept, born of prejudice and fear." He also thought it would be impossible to put into practice, especially keeping black

South Africans out of the cities. "You might as well try to sweep back the sea with a broom," Smuts said. The Nationalists thought such comments only proved that Smuts was unable and unwilling to control the "black peril."

On the night of the election of 1948, Nelson Mandela, now twenty-nine, and his ANC colleagues were at one of their many meetings in Johannesburg. They were deeply involved in arguments about their own policies, and their discussions went on all night. They hardly touched on the election, because they expected Smuts to win.

Early the next morning, when Mandela finally emerged from the meeting, he was shocked to see the newspaper headlines. The Nationalists had won. "South Africa belongs to us once more," Malan announced triumphantly.

CHAPTER 9

APARTHEID TRIUMPHS

SOME ANC MEMBERS THOUGHT IT WOULD NOT make much difference to black South Africans whether Jan Smuts's United Party or Daniel Malan's National Party was in power. But they were wrong.

As quickly as possible, the new government replaced English-speaking officials in all areas of public life—the police, education, the civil service, the military—with the Dutch-heritage Afrikaans speakers. Prime Minister Malan pardoned Robey Leibbrandt, who had been convicted of high treason and sentenced to life imprisonment during World War II. An enthusiastic admirer of Hitler and Nazi Germany, Leibbrandt had been a German secret agent in South Africa.

Parliament began passing apartheid laws. One of the first was the Prohibition of Mixed Marriages Act, intended to keep the white population "pure." Another was the Population Registration Act, requiring that all South Africans be labeled by race. This meant that the government would determine the race of every member of the population, according to four categories: white, Coloured (mixed-race), Indian, or African (black).

However, there was no scientific basis for sorting people by race. Instead the white officials deciding a person's race used ridiculous measurements, like the "pencil test" to judge the curliness of a person's hair. If a pencil stayed in a person's hair, the test went, that person must be African or Coloured; if the pencil fell out, they must be Coloured or white. But the results were no laughing matter. If one parent in a family was judged white and the other parent Coloured, the family could be broken up.

The Group Areas Act decreed that each racial group must live in a separate area. Malan and his Nationalists were especially worried about the social mixing of whites with Indians, biracial people, and blacks. Not very much mixing went on, but the Nationalists feared it would steadily increase.

To many outside the country, as well as to white liberals within South Africa, such unashamed racism was shocking. The Allies had just finished fighting World War II against Nazi Germany, and the world was sickened with revelations from the Third Reich's concentration camps. How could any civilized nation even consider going down that same path?

But the promoters of apartheid believed deeply that the Afrikaners were a special people, to whom God had given this land. By the same token, they believed that black Africans and Asians were inferior peoples who had to be managed. They must either be fenced off in separate areas and strictly controlled, or forced to leave the country.

Watching these frightening developments, Mandela and his friends in the ANC Youth League again looked back on what the African National Congress had accomplished since its founding in 1912. How far had the ANC progressed toward its goals of defending black African rights and working against discrimination? They judged that it had accomplished nothing. Black South Africans had fewer rights, and they suffered worse discrimination, than forty years before. Since the apartheid laws were unjust, the ANC should begin making a deliberate point of breaking those laws.

In December of 1949, the ANC was to hold its annual

conference in Bloemfontein. Before the conference, leaders of the Youth League—Nelson Mandela, Oliver Tambo, Walter Sisulu, and Peter Mda—once again paid a call on Dr. Xuma, president of the ANC. They pointed out that several decades of lawful protests had gotten them nowhere. They urged that the time had come for the kind of passive resistance (illegal but nonviolent) that Gandhi and his followers had used in India. This would mean that leaders of the ANC would have to be willing to break the law and go to jail.

Dr. Xuma completely disagreed with the Youth League. He was sure that the time had *not* yet come for mass action. He feared that if the ANC tried such measures, the Malan government would crush them. And he, personally, was certainly not willing to give up his medical practice and go to prison.

Finally Mandela and the others warned Xuma that if he would not support a program of mass action, they would not support him for re-election as president of the ANC. At that, Xuma became furious. Were they trying to blackmail him? He showed them the door.

The Youth League group began looking for another candidate for president of the ANC. They first approached

Professor Z. K. Matthews, who had helped establish a branch of the Youth League at Fort Hare. But even Matthews thought their ideas were too radical and impractical. They then settled on Dr. James Moroka, who had been a member of the Natives Representative Council. Moroka was sympathetic to the Youth League's ideas, although he didn't know much about the ANC.

At the ANC national conference, Xuma was defeated and Moroka was elected president. Walter Sisulu and Oliver Tambo won key positions. The conference also voted to begin the program of mass action that Mandela and the others urged: boycotts, strikes, civil disobedience, and non-cooperation. When Dr. Xuma resigned from the national executive committee of the ANC, Nelson took his place. Now Mandela was even more deeply involved in the movement.

This ANC national conference was important for the future of South Africa, but it did not get much mention in the white South African press. The white public's attention was focused on the opening of the Voortrekker Monument, a massive granite structure on a hilltop south of Pretoria. The monument commemorated the historic journey of the six thousand Afrikaner pioneers who had left the Cape Colony in the late 1830s. With courage and sacrifice, they had made the Great Trek to the Highveld, the eastern plateau north of the Orange River.

The monument was filled with expressions of Afrikaners' belief that they were destined to rule South Africa. For instance, from the dome high above, a ray of sunlight shone like a divine blessing on words engraved on an upright stone slab: WE FOR THEE, SOUTH AFRICA. These were words from the Afrikaner national hymn, "Die Stem van Suid-Afrika."

The ANC was not the only group working against the apartheid program. Other activists, led by the South African Communist Party and the Transvaal Indian Congress, organized a general strike on May Day, 1950. The purpose of the strike was to protest the laws requiring blacks to carry passes, as well as all the new racist legislation from the Malan government. Mandela and others in the ANC tried to prevent this strike, believing that the communists were trying to upstage the ANC.

One of the young Indians helping to organize the strike was Ahmed Kathrada. He confronted Mandela on the street, accusing him of trying to undermine the strike, and claiming that black South Africans would support it anyway. Mandela was angry at Kathrada that day, although later he came to respect and admire him. But at this point, Mandela was suspicious of any organization that had non-black leaders. He felt that only black South Africans could solve the special problems of black South Africans.

But watching the May Day strike changed Mandela's mind. The strike was so well organized that over two-thirds of African workers stayed home from their jobs and took part in marches. However, the police reacted with violence in four of the townships. In Orlando, where Mandela and Sisulu were trying to get the protesters to disperse, the marchers were charged by the mounted police, and eighteen Africans were shot. Mandela and Sisulu escaped from the gunfire by hiding in a nearby nurses' dormitory.

The government, which was already convinced that communists were a great danger to the nation, passed the Suppression of Communism Act. This act outlawed the South African Communist Party and made it a crime to be a member. But it went much further than that. Because of its vague wording, the Suppression of Communism Act could be interpreted to ban *any* organization opposing the government. Any person, communist or not, who criticized the policies of apartheid could be treated as a criminal.

In response, the ANC joined with the communists and the African People's Organization (an association of so-called Coloured people) to plan a nationwide strike. This national day of protest was to take place on June 26. Mandela worked in the ANC offices in Johannesburg, coordinating the protests by telephone.

This strike was only partially successful, but Mandela felt an inspiring connection with the people all over South Africa who were willing to fight together for their rights. He knew how much the strikers were risking: A striker could lose not only the job he was walking off, but any chance of employment in his industry. In fact, because the pass laws required any black African living in a city to have a job, a striker might also be forced to leave his or her home.

Although Mandela was increasingly drawn into the political struggle, he wished that it did not have to keep him from his family. Nelson and Evelyn's second son, Makgatho Lewanika, was born in the middle of the protest. Nelson did manage to be at the hospital when the baby was born, but only briefly. Fortunately his mother, Nosekeni Fanny, had come to Johannesburg the year before and joined the household, so she was on hand to help Evelyn.

But Nelson Mandela missed his family. It struck his heart when Evelyn told him that Thembi, five years old, had asked her, "Where does Daddy live?" Day after day, Mandela had left the house before dawn and come home late at night, after Thembi was asleep. It was no wonder the little boy had gotten the impression that Daddy, whom he hardly ever saw, must live somewhere else.

It did not help that Evelyn was more and more opposed to Mandela's political activities. She did not believe that politics were important, and she was angry that they took him away from home so much. In contrast, Walter Sisulu's wife, Albertina, supported him wholeheartedly. Walter had decided to work full-time for the ANC, giving up his real estate business, and the family was living on Albertina's salary as a nurse.

Since Mandela needed to travel so often for the ANC, he decided to learn to drive and get his driver's license. He enjoyed car trips through the countryside with the windows rolled down, and good ideas often came to him while he was gazing out the window. One day, however, as he drove through the farmland northeast of Bloemfontein, he ran out of gas.

Walking to the nearest farm, Mandela asked to buy some gasoline. But the white farm woman shut the door in his face. Maybe she was offended by Mandela's confident manner; maybe she feared he was dangerous. In any case, Mandela had to trudge to the next farm, two miles away.

By the time he reached the second farmhouse, he had made up his mind to play the humble role that Afrikaner farmers expected of a black man. He would pretend to be the servant of a white employer. Trying to look humble, Mandela said to the farmer, "My *baas* has run out of petrol." Using the word *baas*, meaning "boss" or "master" in Afrikaans, showed that this black man knew his "proper" place.

The farmer gave him the gas, and Mandela went on his way. He had done the practical thing, but it bothered him that he had used the degrading word *baas*. That farmer had seemed friendly. Maybe he would have sold Mandela the gas even if he had asked, in a dignified way, for himself.

In the spring of 1951, the Malan government launched the Separate Registration of Voters Act, intended to take voting rights away from the Coloureds of the Cape Province. In the Cape Province, especially in Cape Town, Coloured citizens had had the unusual right to vote along with white citizens since the nineteenth century. Naturally, they had voted against Malan in the 1948 election. It was becoming more and more obvious that the National Party's apartheid policies were affecting the blacks, Indians, and Coloureds of South Africa alike. It made sense for all those groups to work together.

In January 1952 the leaders of the African National Congress wrote to Prime Minister Malan, demanding repeal of the apartheid laws. If the laws were not repealed, they warned, they would launch a Defiance Campaign, the nationwide disobedience of apartheid laws. Malan's secretary wrote back that they would certainly not repeal the laws, and that any disobedience would be promptly punished.

The ANC planned the starting date of their Defiance Campaign for June 26. Traveling around South Africa before the Defiance Campaign, Nelson Mandela spoke to groups of volunteers. In Durban, a city on the east coast, Mandela stood before a crowd of ten thousand black Africans and Indians. He was thrilled to address such a large audience, and he was moved to see Africans and Indians joining forces against apartheid.

Their purpose, Mandela told his audience, would be to deliberately disobey apartheid laws. Some of them would enter railway coaches or restrooms marked NET BLANKES, WHITES ONLY. Some would remain in the city after the special curfew for nonwhites. Some would walk into a post office through the entrance reserved for whites. The leaders would inform the police in advance of the protests, so that they could arrest the protesters peacefully if they wished.

Mandela explained to his audiences how important it was to keep the protests nonviolent, even if the government responded with force. Part of the aim of the protests was to arouse sympathy for the people oppressed by apartheid, and they would lose sympathy if they were violent. Besides, violence on the part of the protesters would give the government an excuse to crush them with all their military power.

On the first day of the Defiance Campaign, the protests and the arrests went as planned. Walter Sisulu was arrested as he led a group without the proper entry permits into the African area of Boksburg, near Johannesburg. Nelson Mandela was in Johannesburg itself, observing the protests, but he did not plan to get arrested yet.

That night, after a meeting downtown, Mandela walked

out onto the street and was suddenly faced with a police-man. The policeman gestured with his nightstick toward a waiting police van. Mandela thought of explaining to the policeman that he was not scheduled to be arrested until later in the campaign, but clearly the policeman would not get the joke. There was nothing to do but climb into the van with the other protesters. On the way to the police station, the protesters' spirits were high, and they sang the African anthem, "Nkosi Sikelel' iAfrika."

The arrested men, more than fifty of them including Mandela, were herded into a yard at the police station. One of Mandela's companions, pushed by a guard, fell down some steps and broke his ankle. Mandela demanded medical care for the man, but the guards refused to notify a doctor until the next day. The prisoner moaned in pain all night.

After two days in prison, Mandela was released on bail. The Defiance Campaign continued for six months, with great success. The national membership of the ANC swelled from twenty thousand to one hundred thousand. Nelson Mandela took these results as proof that all the peoples labeled as "inferior" by apartheid needed to work together.

However, the Nationalist government did not react

A traditional rondavel, like the one that Nelson Mandela lived in as a child, in Transkei, Eastern Cape, South Africa

Nelson Mandela in 1950

As a young man, Nelson took up boxing. He continued to practice the sport even while in prison.

Nelson Mandela as a young lawyer in his office

Nelson Mandela and Winnie Madikizela at their wedding in 1957

The entrance to the prison on Robben Island, where Mandela would spend so many years, and the limestone quarry where he and others labored. On February 10, 1995, Mandela visited his former cell in the notorious prison.

Newspaper headlines heralded Mandela's release in 1990.

Nelson and Winnie salute the crowds after his release from prison.

Nelson Mandela and F. W. de Klerk give a press conference during their negotiations at CODESA (the Convention for a Democratic South Africa) in 1990.

African National Congress (ANC) leader Nelson Mandela and general secretary Walter Sisulu attend a rally in Soweto on February 13, 1990.

Nelson Mandela presents the Springboks rugby team with their championship trophy. Mandela's embrace of the Springboks was important to the easing of racial tensions in post–apartheid South Africa.

Nelson Mandela holds the Jules Rimet Trophy on May 15, 2004. South Africa won the right to host the 2010 World Cup finals, the first to be played in Africa.

Nelson Mandela and his third wife, Graça Machel.

On his ninety-fourth birthday, Nelson Mandela posed for a photograph with his former wife Winnie Madikizela-Mandela and their daughters, Zindzi and Zenani, at his home in Qunu, South Africa.

© Getty Images

© Getty Images

On December 10, 2013, dignitaries and regular South African citizens gathered together to celebrate the life of Nelson Mandela at a public memorial service at the FNB Stadium in Johannesburg, South Africa.

to the Defiance Campaign the way Mandela had hoped. Instead of agreeing to negotiate with the protesters, they clamped down harder. Parliament passed the Public Safety Act, which allowed the government to hold people in prison without trial. They also passed the Criminal Law Amendment Act, which allowed corporal punishments, such as flogging.

In July 1952, when the Defiance Campaign was in full swing, the police raided the offices of the ANC. They arrested twenty-one of its Johannesburg leaders, including Nelson Mandela and Walter Sisulu, for the crime of "statutory communism." They ransacked the offices for papers that might be used as evidence against them. Leaders of the Transvaal Indian Congress, including Ahmed Kathrada, were also arrested and charged, and so were campaign directors around the country. The government was determined to make an example of these leaders.

CHAPTER 10
DEFIANCE

NELSON MANDELA WAS NOT AT ALL INTIMIDATED BY his arrest during the Defiance Campaign. His law career was taking off. Although he had given up on getting a law degree, he passed the qualifying exam to become an attorney, and he applied to join the Transvaal Law Society. Mandela's former employer, Lazar Sidelsky, gladly gave him a recommendation to the Society, but he warned him again about politics. "You'll end up in jail sooner or later," Sidelsky predicted.

Later in 1952, while Mandela was out on bail and awaiting trial for his Defiance Campaign actions, he and Oliver Tambo opened the first black South African law firm. MANDELA AND TAMBO, as the sign on the window of their office announced, was located in downtown Johannesburg, opposite the magistrates' courts. The location was important for two reasons: because it was close to the courts, and because most of their clients worked in Johannesburg.

This location would soon be declared a "whites only" area, forbidden to black-owned businesses. By law, Mandela and Tambo should then have moved to a black township several miles out of town, completely inconvenient for them and their clients. However, they managed to stay downtown until 1961.

Oliver Tambo and Nelson Mandela made a good team. Tambo was quiet, thoughtful, and logical. Mandela was dramatic and emotional; he liked to cause a stir. Therefore Tambo usually did the background work in the office, while Mandela appeared in court to plead the cases.

Almost as soon as the Mandela and Tambo law firm opened their doors, they had more business than they could handle. This was understandable, since many attorneys would not represent black clients, and the ones who would charged blacks higher rates. Clients eager to see Mandela and Tambo crowded the waiting room and stood in long lines on the stairway and in the halls. The ANC made Mandela and Tambo their official attorneys.

Mandela was inspired by the plight of the people he

worked for. The net of apartheid laws bound blacks so tightly that it was hard for them *not* to commit a crime. It was illegal not to have a job, and illegal to have a job reserved for white men. It was illegal not to carry a pass book, and it was illegal to possess a pass book without an employer's signature. Once they were charged with a crime, black people were assumed to be guilty. The courts routinely punished them with fines, imprisonment, and even whipping.

Mandela and Tambo handled the same kinds of cases over and over: A black farmer was evicted from the land his family had worked for generations. An impoverished old black woman was arrested for brewing beer at home to make a little money. A black maid was accused by her employer of stealing clothes.

Nelson Mandela, attorney-at-law, made a striking figure in the courtroom. He was six feet two inches tall, with broad shoulders and a noble bearing. He was always well dressed.

Mandela made a point of ignoring some of the many insulting apartheid restrictions—for instance, he would stride into the courtroom through the "whites only" entrance. He had come a long way from his first year in

124

Johannesburg, when he took his tea break in the office kitchen to avoid confronting the white secretaries' racism. His cases became known for their entertainment value, and the spectators' gallery was usually full.

Mandela relished theatrical flourishes. In the case of the maid accused of stealing her employer's clothes, he confronted the employer, a white woman, in cross-examination. The evidence, the clothes that supposedly had been stolen, was displayed in the court.

Mandela walked over to the evidence table, picked up a pair of women's underpants on the tip of his pencil, and turned to the white woman. "Madam, are these . . . yours?" he asked. The woman was too embarrassed to claim the underpants in public, and the case was finally dismissed.

At one trial, when Mandela represented a black clerk accused of fraud, the judge was aggressively racist. He challenged Mandela's credentials as an attorney, interrupted him constantly, and finally ordered him out of the courtroom. With the help of George Bizos, one of Mandela's white friends from law school, Mandela petitioned the Supreme Court to remove the judge from the case. Luckily, the Supreme Court case came before Quartus de Wet, a fair-minded judge who had been appointed before the

Nationalists came to power. The racist judge was forced to withdraw.

Since the arrest in July 1952 of Mandela, Sisulu, J. B. Marks, Dr. Yusuf Dadoo, Dr. Moroka, and the rest of the twenty-one for "promoting communism," they had been out on bail. In November the case finally came to trial. As the law now defined communism, there was plenty of evidence to convict the defendants of "statutory communism." However, the judge was reasonable, and he admitted, "This has nothing to do with communism as it is commonly known." Noting that the defendants had led a peaceful protest and consistently urged nonviolence to their followers, he gave them a suspended sentence.

Mandela's satisfaction with this outcome was spoiled by the behavior of Dr. Moroka, president of the ANC, during the trial. Mandela felt that Moroka should have set an example of courage and defiance. But Moroka refused to even be associated with the other defendants, especially the members of the South African Communist Party. Worst of all, on the witness stand, Moroka claimed that he did not believe in racial equality. Mandela and his friends were appalled.

In December, the month after the trial, the ANC annual

conference elected a new president, the widely respected Albert Luthuli. Luthuli, fifty-three years old, was a Zulu chief, chosen by his tribal elders in 1936, and a leader in the Natal branch of the ANC. He was also a devout Christian, committed to nonviolence. He had served on the Natives Representative Council, that "toy telephone" for blacks, so he had learned how useless it was to protest injustice through official channels. When the apartheid government ordered Luthuli to either resign from the ANC or give up his government-controlled chieftainship, he stayed in the ANC.

Nelson Mandela thought Luthuli was a good choice for president, but he could not attend the ANC national conference that year. He had been "banned." Banning was a tool used by the apartheid government to control the movements of a person without actually imprisoning him or her. Mandela, as well as fifty-one other leaders of the ANC, was banned for six months, forbidden to go any-where outside the Johannesburg district. He also could not attend any meetings or gatherings of more than one person, so he could not make any public speeches. In fact, the government had so restricted Mandela with bans that he could not even attend the birthday party of one of his children.

• • •

In spite of the bans, the ANC leaders managed to meet in secret. Mandela warned his colleagues that any day now the government would outlaw the ANC itself. Therefore, they should be prepared to go underground.

The apartheid laws that had already been passed were oppressive, but they were only the beginning of the Nationalist government's master plan for apartheid in South Africa. Since 1950 the minister of native affairs, and the designer of the master plan, had been Hendrik Verwoerd. Verwoerd, a deceptively soft-spoken man with a kindly face, presented apartheid as best for blacks as well as whites. As citizens of their reserves rather than of South Africa, he explained, blacks could develop separately according to their tribal traditions.

Verwoerd called apartheid "a policy of good neighborliness." It was actually a plan under which white people would not have any black neighbors at all. In Johannesburg, the plan included the Western Areas Removal.

The purpose of this program was to erase any so-called "black spots," the areas in cities where black people still owned property. The most obvious such area in Johannesburg was Sophiatown, near the center of the city. Sophiatown housed some 54,000 black residents, as well as Asians and

Coloureds. Many of them existed in squalor—the reason blacks had been allowed to buy here in the first place was that it was next to a sewage dump. But some, like Dr. Xuma, lived in comfortable homes. Sophiatown boasted an exciting nightlife of music and dance, and it had the only swimming pool for blacks in all of Johannesburg.

In 1953 the government prepared to put the Western Areas Removal program into effect. They intended to remove all 54,000 black residents of Sophiatown and resettle them on Meadowlands, a stretch of flat land nine miles from the city center. Besides uprooting so many people from their homes, the removal would cause a serious hardship for those who commuted to jobs in the city.

The new township, Meadowlands, would be regulated by the city government, with a fenced border like Orlando. It would have no shops or businesses. No residents would be allowed to own their homes; the apartheid attitude was that blacks did not belong in the cities, except as temporary workers. Their true homes, according to Verwoerd's ideas, were in the native reserves under the rule of tribal chiefs.

The ANC was outraged by the Western Areas Removals plan. To rally resistance, the ANC held meetings every week in Freedom Square in Sophiatown. When it was Mandela's turn to speak one night, he got carried away. He said that the time for passive resistance was over, and that apartheid could only be destroyed by violence. He encouraged the crowd to sing a freedom song that went, "There are the enemies; let us take our weapons and attack them."

The executive committee of the ANC heard about Mandela's fiery speech, and they were very angry. Chief Luthuli and Z. K. Matthews told Mandela that he was recklessly endangering not only his audience, but also the ANC itself. In any case, by September of 1954 Mandela was again under government bans, and he was unable to attend meetings or give speeches.

But Mandela was becoming more and more convinced that nonviolent civil disobedience would not work in South Africa. Nonviolence, Mandela believed, had worked against the British government in India because the British were realistic and farsighted. The Nationalists in South Africa, however, believed so deeply in apartheid that they didn't hesitate to use violence to enforce it. As Hendrik Verwoerd put it, "I do not have the nagging doubt of ever wondering whether perhaps I am wrong."

In the end, the ANC could not prevent the government from removing Sophiatown. In February 1955 the government sent trucks and armed policemen into Sophiatown and began transporting residents and their belongings out to Meadowlands. When a section had been emptied, the bulldozers moved in to raze the buildings. After the entire community had been cleared, developers began construction on a new suburb for whites. They named it Triomf, Afrikaans for "triumph."

Back in 1953, the Department of Native Affairs had turned its attention to education for black South Africans. Up until now, the only education available for blacks had been the mission schools, most of them established and run by English-speaking churches. Less than half of black South Africans received any schooling. But still, it was possible for a few lucky black children, as Nelson had been, to attend school all the way through university and become as well educated as any whites.

Minister of Native Affairs Verwoerd was determined to change this system. He explained that it was a mistake to allow teachers who believed in racial equality, such as some of the British missionaries, to educate "Natives." Likewise, it was a mistake to offer higher education to any black South Africans. Since under apartheid blacks would only be allowed to hold such jobs as household servants or ditch-diggers, they should receive only enough education to do this menial work. If blacks were taught such advanced subjects as mathematics, they might form unrealistic expectations about their place in life, become disappointed, and cause trouble. These ideas were all summed up in the Bantu Education Act of 1953.

Verwoerd often used the term "Bantu" to refer to South African blacks. The Bantu were a group of tribes with related languages who had gradually migrated from the north into South Africa over many centuries. However, Verwoerd deliberately called black South Africans "Bantu" to underline his insistence that they really belonged only to their tribes, not to the nation of South Africa.

The Bantu Education Act took control of the mission schools away from the churches. As Verwoerd described the new system, "Natives will be taught from childhood to realize that equality with Europeans is not for them." Nelson Mandela described "Bantu education" even more bluntly as "an inferior type of education, designed to relegate Africans to a position of perpetual servitude."

Meanwhile, Mandela's enemies were trying to prevent

him from practicing law. In 1954 the Transvaal Law Society petitioned the Supreme Court to remove Mandela from its roll of accredited attorneys. They claimed that Mandela's political activity amounted to dishonorable and unprofessional conduct. However, the justice who heard the case disagreed, and Mandela continued to pursue his career.

Nelson Mandela was doing very well in many ways. He was widely admired for his leadership of the protests against apartheid. He was physically fit, working out regularly at an Orlando community center. Boxing was his favorite sport, and during his Johannesburg years Mandela had put on weight and become more muscular, so he was now in the heavyweight class. His legal business was thriving, and he was able to pay for tailored suits and buy himself a large, impressive Oldsmobile.

One rainy, blustery night, as he drove past a bus stop, Mandela noticed his former employer, Lazar Sidelsky, waiting for a bus. Giving Sidelsky a ride home, Mandela reminded him of the time that he had loaned Mandela seventy-five pounds. Sidelsky refused to discuss the loan, but a few days later he received a check in the mail from Mandela for seventy-five pounds.

Nelson Mandela's career might be flourishing, but his

family life was falling apart. Evelyn had never approved of Nelson's involvement in politics, and she clung to the dream that he would someday give it up. She did not even want to live in Johannesburg; she hoped they would move back to the Transkei. Kaiser Matanzima was still trying to persuade Mandela to return, and she encouraged him.

Evelyn became increasingly religious, and she prayed for another girl child to replace the one who had died. In 1954 Evelyn and Nelson's second daughter, named Makaziwe after the first, was born. Evelyn took this as a sign from God, and shortly afterward she joined the Jehovah's Witnesses, who are forbidden to take part in political activity. She took the children to church with her and even tried to convert Nelson to her faith.

But there was no chance that Nelson Mandela would give up politics. Furthermore, he wanted his children to understand how important the political struggle in South Africa was. He hung pictures of his heroes—Winston Churchill, Franklin Roosevelt, Stalin, Mahatma Gandhi—in the house. He pointed them out to Thembi and Makgatho as he explained what these great people had done. By this time, Evelyn and Nelson were hardly speaking to each other.

Mandela and other ANC leaders decided that it was

not enough to combat apartheid laws, such as the Western Areas Removal program or the Bantu Education Act, one at a time. Apartheid was an all-encompassing system, blighting every aspect of life for black South Africans, and so the ANC must offer an all-encompassing vision of hope. In 1955 Professor Z. K. Matthews proposed that they convene a national congress for this purpose. They would invite all the people of South Africa, and they would present a Freedom Charter "for the democratic South Africa of the future."

The assembly that ratified the Freedom Charter met on a football field in Kliptown, several miles outside Johannesburg, on June 26. The excited, optimistic gathering of three thousand included whites, Coloureds, and Asians as well as blacks. Nelson Mandela and Walter Sisulu were there—illegally, since they were banned to remain in Johannesburg. They knew that Special Branch detectives, the secret police, were watching the crowd, so they stayed on the outskirts.

The Freedom Charter was a remarkable document, with ideas contributed by thousands of people from all over the country. It declared, to begin with, that "South Africa belongs to all who live in it, black and white, and that no government can justly claim authority unless it is based on the will of the people." Each man and woman in South Africa was entitled to vote for the government of their choice. All apartheid laws must be repealed, and all people must have equal rights, regardless of race, national origin, or gender.

On the second day of the congress, the police raided the assembly, announcing that treason was suspected. The football field was cordoned off, and the police began taking down the names of each delegate. Mandela left before he could be arrested and thrown in jail for breaking the ban on him.

But the congress had already ratified each section of the Freedom Charter. The Freedom Charter was nonracist, noncommunist, and inclusive of all national origins. It did not claim South Africa for black Africans only. It did not promote revolution, as many white people feared. This document, like the Declaration of Independence by the thirteen American colonies, would be a powerful touchstone for years to come.

In September 1955 the bans preventing Nelson Mandela from traveling or attending meetings expired. He was no longer restricted to Johannesburg. Quickly, before the government could slap another ban on him, he headed for the Transkei. He missed the open countryside, the rolling hills of his childhood. The night before he left Orlando, two-year-old Makaziwe woke up and asked if she could come along on her father's trip. Tucking his toddler back into bed, Mandela felt guilty and sad. He was reminded again of how little time he spent with his children these days.

On his way to the Transkei, Mandela made stops in Natal to meet with regional ANC leaders, including Chief Luthuli. From the port of Durban, he drove south along the coast and then inland, into the Transkei. In between his political business, he stopped in Qunu, the village of his childhood. He visited his mother and tried to persuade her to come live with him in Johannesburg for good. But Nosekeni Fanny would not leave the countryside.

Mandela had a happier visit in Qunu with his sister Mabel, now married. She was practical and easygoing and was his favorite sister. He went on to Mqhekezweni, where his foster mother, No-England, welcomed him with great excitement.

Mandela's business in the Transkei was especially concerned with the Bantu Authorities. That was the system that Verwoerd, the minister of native affairs, was trying to impose on the tribal areas. Supposedly the new system would allow each tribe to develop along their own lines, ruled by their chiefs and educating their children in their own language.

But the ANC thought that the Bantu Authorities were only a way for the white government to divide and control the black peoples of South Africa. The chiefs would be chosen and paid by the government, and there would be no representatives elected by the people. Mandela's foster brother, Justice Dalindyebo, had already been ousted from his chieftainship by the apartheid government.

Mandela found himself on the opposite side of this issue from his old friend and cousin Kaiser Matanzima. Matanzima agreed with the Verwoerd government that it was important for each tribe to preserve their customs and tribal leadership. The Bantu Authorities plan would benefit him, since by birth he was in line to be chief of a large section of the Thembu. He thought that the ANC's resistance to apartheid would only result in bloodshed.

Matanzima and Mandela debated this issue before the

tribal council, but it was clear that neither would change the other's mind. Mandela loved and respected Matanzima, and he was deeply sad that they could not agree.

A few months later Mandela returned to the Transkei to buy a piece of land in Umtata. He had come a long way from his roots in Qunu and Mqhekezweni, but at least he could own a bit of this earth.

CHAPTER 11
TRAITOR OR PATRIOT?

VERY EARLY ONE MORNING IN DECEMBER 1956, THE
Mandela household woke up to pounding on the door. The
Special Branch officer outside had a warrant for Nelson's
arrest. The charge was high treason, for which the punish-
ment was death. With his children watching, the police took
Mandela away to the main Johannesburg prison.

Mandela and 120 other black leaders of the ANC, and
of antiapartheid movements from other parts of South
Africa, were locked up in two cells. The floors were
cement, there was no furniture, and the latrines were open
holes in the floor. Each prisoner was given a sleeping mat
and thin blankets infested with lice. A few white prisoners,
including Joe Slovo and Ruth First, had also been arrested,
but they were kept in more comfortable cells with mat-
tresses and clean blankets.

Even under these dismal living conditions, Mandela was glad to be with his fellow activists. After years of being forbidden to meet, they could now meet twenty-four hours a day. They had long political discussions, they sang freedom songs, and they did exercises to keep fit. They even danced a Zulu war dance, led by Chief Luthuli.

Some of these men were from the cities, some from the country; some were young and some were older. They had loyalties to various tribes. But here they felt a close bond with one another: They were all South African patriots.

After two weeks, the prisoners were taken into court to hear the charges against them. Large crowds gathered outside to cheer, as if they were heroes rather than accused criminals. When they walked into the courtroom, the nonwhite section of the gallery cheered them again. Mandela and his friends smiled, giving the ANC raised-fist salute.

On the second day of reading the charges, the prisoners entered the courtroom to find a wire cage set up for them to sit in. One prisoner wrote a sarcastic sign and fastened it to the side of the cage: DANGEROUS. PLEASE DO

NOT FEED. The defense team protested the cage vigorously, and finally the judge ordered it taken down.

After the evidence had been presented, Nelson Mandela was freed on bail until his trial, and he went home. But he found the house empty. Evelyn had taken the children and moved in with her brother in Orlando East.

A year earlier, in December 1955, Evelyn had confronted Nelson with an either-or choice: Choose family, or choose politics. Much as he loved his children, Mandela could not make this choice. He had tried to explain to Evelyn that the ANC's struggle for freedom in South Africa was not just an activity that he could pick up or put down. It was his "lifework," "an essential and fundamental part" of his being.

Sometime after Evelyn left, Mandela filed for divorce. Thembi, Makgatho, and Makaziwe were all distressed by their parents' failed marriage, but Thembi was the hardest hit. He became extremely quiet, and he seemed to lose interest in school. Mandela made sure to spend time with Thembi, taking him jogging and to the gym. But as the boy grew older, he blamed his father for the family breakup.

Meanwhile, the preparation for the Treason Trial dragged on throughout 1957. Mandela was served with a new ban, confining him to Johannesburg for the next five years and forbidding him to attend meetings. The ban made it more difficult for him to practice law, since many of Mandela and Tambo's clients lived in rural areas. The once-thriving law practice of Mandela and Tambo slowed almost to a halt.

During this period Nelson Mandela met a young woman named Winnie Nomzamo Madikizela. She was from Bizana in Pondoland, the same district of the Transkei where Oliver Tambo had grown up. She had come to Johannesburg to study in a school for social workers. She was only twenty-two, while Mandela was thirty-eight, but she was smart, beautiful, and spirited.

In spite of a troubled childhood, Winnie had done well in school. For the past two years she had been a social worker at Baragwanath Hospital, where she was known for her cheerfulness and concern for other people. Mandela was smitten with her, and she was awed by the attentions of such a well-known attorney and defendant in the Treason Trial. She was impressed, as many people were, that he carried himself like a hereditary chief.

From the very first time Winnie went out with Nelson

Mandela, it was obvious what his personal life was like: full of constant interruptions from politics. Mandela took her to lunch at an Indian restaurant near his office, and a stream of people came by their table, wanting to talk to him about political matters. Out on the sidewalk after lunch, it seemed to Winnie that every few feet someone stopped Mandela to talk.

After Mandela's divorce from Evelyn, he and Winnie were married in June 1958. Because of his ban to Johannesburg, Mandela had to get special permission to travel to Winnie's hometown, Bizana, where the wedding took place. There were several members of the secret police, uninvited, among the guests at the reception.

Winnie's stern father gave a speech foreseeing rocky times ahead for the couple: "This marriage will be no bed of roses; it is threatened from all sides and only the deepest love will preserve it." Mandela had already warned Winnie that they would probably have to live on her salary as a social worker, but that turned out to be the least of their problems.

Shortly after their wedding, Winnie and Nelson were awakened one night by banging on the front door and lights flashing in the windows. Winnie was frightened, but

Mandela told her not to be alarmed—it was only a police raid. The Afrikaner policemen clumped into the house and began searching, dumping out drawers of clothes, pulling books off shelves, and reading personal mail, all the while commenting with racial slurs. Winnie was disgusted, but Mandela told her she would have to get used to such raids. It was part of the political struggle he was engaged in.

Winnie had not been much interested in politics before meeting Mandela, but she took up the struggle against apartheid as her own. She accepted Mandela's political friends enthusiastically, especially Oliver Tambo, whom she had already admired, and Ismail and Fatima Meer, Indians who lived in Durban. Before long, Winnie joined the women's movement against apartheid.

The latest development in the government's apartheid plan was to make women, as well as men, carry pass books. Winnie refused publicly, and she even struck a policeman who tried to serve her with a summons. The policeman charged her with assault, but Mandela's friend George Bizos defended her in court, and the charges were dropped.

In September of 1958 Hendrik Verwoerd, the master planner of apartheid, was elected prime minister of South Africa. "I believe that the will of God was revealed in the ballot," he said of the election results. His victory may have had more to do with the fact that only white people—less than half the population of the country—were allowed to vote.

Verwoerd was bent on further separating the black peoples of South Africa from one another, as well as completely separating them from whites. The Promotion of Bantu Self-Government Act of 1959, following up on the earlier Bantu Authorities Act, created eight "Bantustans," or separate homelands, for the black tribes. Every black person in South Africa would have citizenship and political rights only in their own homeland. Each Bantustan would be ruled by a chief, but the chief would be responsible to the white government. This arrangement would prevent the black majority of South Africa from uniting against the white minority.

Under "Bantu Self-Government," black people who lived in the cities, even if they had lived there for generations, would be considered as members of their tribe of origin and citizens of their "homeland." They would need special permits to work in "white" areas. The absurdity of this law was that two-thirds of black adults could not *afford* to reside in their supposed homelands, because these areas were much too small and poor. Even more than in the past, blacks could not earn a living in the reserves, and they were forced to seek jobs in the cities.

"Bantu Self-Government" and other apartheid policies seemed so wildly unreasonable that many people, inside and outside South Africa, thought they were bound to break down. Many ANC leaders believed that even the white population was sure to realize that apartheid was unworkable, as well as unjust. Walter Sisulu had written in 1957 that the National Party had "reached its high-water mark." Chief Luthuli was greatly heartened when white liberals organized a defense fund for the accused in the Treason Trial; he took it as a sign that white resistance to the apartheid government was growing.

However, another faction of the ANC refused to count on whites, liberal or not, for anything. For some time there had been a fiercely debated split in the ANC. On the one hand, there were those like Nelson Mandela, Walter Sisulu, and Oliver Tambo, who thought all races should be included in a new South Africa. On the other hand there were the Africanists, who thought South Africa should be for black people only.

In April 1959 the Africanists left the ANC and formed

their own party, the Pan-Africanist Congress (PAC). Robert Sobukwe, a dedicated leader of the ANC Youth League, was elected president of the PAC. He was anticommunist as well as Africanist, fearing that white and Indian communists had come to dominate the ANC.

The PAC announced its intention to overthrow the white supremacy and establish an Africanist government in South Africa. Whites and even Indians, they declared, were "aliens" who had no place in the country. Communists, an international group led by whites, were also unwelcome. The PAC promised that under their program, black liberation in South Africa would be accomplished by 1963. It was a very attractive idea, although Mandela was sure that such a speedy victory was impossible.

The PAC was encouraged by the momentous events taking place in other African countries. One after the other, former European colonies moved toward independence. Ghana, a country on the central west coast of Africa, had already become independent from Britain in 1957.

But in Ghana, as in Nigeria, Congo, Tanganyika, and most other countries of Africa, the population was overwhelmingly black. Therefore, independence naturally meant black rule. In South Africa, however, whites were a large minority—almost one third of the population. And those of Dutch descent, the Afrikaners, had deep roots in the country. Mandela, Sisulu, and other ANC leaders were convinced that the various races in South Africa must cooperate in order to bring about a just and peaceful society.

On February 4, 1959, Winnie and Mandela's first child, a daughter named Zenani, was born. Mandela was able to drive Winnie to the hospital, but not to stay there for the birth. He had to appear in court for the Treason Trial, which had been moved to Pretoria. Pretoria was thirty-six miles north of Johannesburg, a two-hour bus trip each way.

This distance was a hardship on Mandela and the rest of the defendants and their lawyers, who had to spend more time and money traveling to the courtroom every day. Mandela and Tambo's law practice was already suffering from the partners' absence. Also, their many supporters in Johannesburg would not be able to attend the trial. That was the main reason the courts had moved the trial, to avoid allowing the defendants a large, enthusiastic audience in the courtroom.

However, the prisoners developed a close bond with one another merely from sitting together in the courtroom day after day. Although they were racially segregated in their prison cells, in court they were seated in alphabetical order. The defendants seemed to demonstrate in person the Freedom Charter's call for a multiracial society.

The pretrial business of the Treason Trial was dragged out until August 1959, when the actual trial began. All the defendants pleaded not guilty. For the first two months of the trial, the police presented their evidence gathered from raiding the prisoners' homes and offices.

The prosecuting attorney had promised to show evidence that the prisoners planned to overthrow the government of South Africa by violence and replace it with a communist state. But many items of evidence, such as wedding invitations, or signs labeling the soup in the lunch line at the Freedom Charter congress, had nothing to do with the charges. From August through December and on into 1960, the prosecution presented evidence and witnesses, finally concluding early in March.

While the ANC leaders accused in the Treason Trial began their defense, the Pan-African Congress (PAC) launched a nationwide protest against the pass laws. The idea was for all workers to arrive at their police stations refusing to carry passes. If enough blacks participated, the police departments would be overwhelmed.

The PAC was poorly organized, but even so the protest was effective in Sharpeville, a black township south of the Witwatersrand. About five thousand Africans showed up at the police station on the morning of March 21, 1960, and refused to leave. Early in the afternoon, a scuffle broke out near the front of the crowd. The police panicked and opened fire without warning. The crowd scattered, but sixty-seven blacks were killed—most of them shot in the back—and 186 wounded.

The ANC thought the PAC had used poor judgment in launching the protest without proper planning, but they followed up by announcing a national day of mourning on March 28. Chief Luthuli publicly burned his pass, and so did Mandela. Around South Africa thousands of blacks did likewise, and in Cape Town thirty thousand Africans marched to protest police brutality. Many blacks were hopeful that liberation was at hand.

Outside South Africa, newspapers published photos of the protests and shootings, and international opinion turned against the apartheid government. The United Nations condemned South Africa's racial policies, and so did the United States government. The British prime minister, Harold Macmillan, had visited South Africa the month before and tried to get Verwoerd to reconsider, but without any success. Macmillan's term for Verwoerd's position was "fanaticism."

Instead of reconsidering their policies, the apartheid government moved swiftly to crack down on the protesters. On March 28, 1960, the same date as the ANC's day of mourning for the Sharpeville massacre, the Unlawful Organizations Act was introduced in Parliament. As the minister of justice explained, this legislation would allow the government to outlaw the ANC, the PAC, and any other organization with similar aims, and stop their "reign of terror." The government declared a state of emergency, and the country was now under martial law.

In the middle of the night on March 31, the police arrived at the Mandelas' house without a warrant. Under martial law, they did not need any authorization to invade a private residence, to search Nelson Mandela's home, or to seize him and carry him off to prison.

Nelson Mandela was not the only one arrested without a warrant that night. He and thirty-nine others were crammed into a bare, filthy cell at the Sophiatown prison and held there for a day and a half. Then they were transferred from Johannesburg to Pretoria, to be held in Pretoria Local Prison while the Treason Trial proceeded.

From the first, Mandela refused to accept disrespectful treatment from the guards and wardens. When a guard shouted at him to remove his hands from his pockets, Mandela left his hands where they were. When a Special Branch detective called him "Nelson," Mandela answered, "I am not 'Nelson' to you; I am Mr. Mandela." When the cells at Pretoria Local Prison turned out to be as cramped and foul as those in Sophiatown, Mandela complained to the commanding officer.

"You have brought the vermin into my prison from your filthy homes," retorted the officer. However, shortly afterward the cells were painted and fumigated, and the prisoners were given clean blankets. The prisoners in the Treason Trial were also given a larger cell. They were allowed to keep law books, in order to prepare their defense.

This time, Oliver Tambo was not among the prisoners. By agreement among the leaders of the ANC, he had

153

left the country just before the state of emergency was proclaimed. They could see that the ANC would soon be declared illegal. One of them needed to be free to work for the ANC outside South Africa.

Tambo was driven north to the border of Bechuanaland (later Botswana) by Ronald Segal, the white editor of a liberal journal. From there Tambo escaped to Ghana. He would spend most of the rest of his life in exile.

CHAPTER 12
THE TROUBLEMAKER

IN PRETORIA, NELSON MANDELA CONTINUED TO protest the conditions of the black prisoners. Apartheid laws applied to the prison system, too, sometimes to ridiculous extremes. At first the black prisoners were not given any sugar or bread, although the Indian, Coloured, and white prisoners did receive these foods. Furthermore, the white prisoners were given *white* sugar and *white* bread, while the Indians and Coloured prisoners were given *brown* sugar and *brown* bread. After Mandela and his cellmates complained, the black prisoners received what was called an Improved Diet—they were given bread with their meals.

The court allowed Mandela to travel to Johannesburg, under guard, to close up the law firm of Mandela and Tambo. He spent his days in the office and his nights in the local jail. The police sergeant guarding him was a decent man, and he allowed Mandela to go to the café downstairs for lunch. He even pretended not to notice when Winnie arrived there to see her husband.

In Pretoria, the state of emergency restrictions made it almost impossible for the defense lawyers to consult with their clients and prepare a case. And the prison regulations, separating white from black and men from women, made it almost as difficult for the defendants to consult with one another. The prison authorities finally allowed such mixed consultations, but only with the races and genders separated by a complicated set of iron grilles. Mandela and the other defendants worked together as best they could for five months.

During this period, Winnie visited Mandela in prison several times, bringing Zenani, nicknamed Zeni, with her. Mandela was delighted to hold their little daughter and kiss her, but it was always painful to say good-bye. Zeni was just beginning to walk and talk, and as she left with her mother, she would motion her father to come along with them. There was no way to explain to her that he could not.

At the beginning of August, it was Mandela's turn to give testimony. The prosecution attempted to prove that he was a violent communist. Mandela, for his part, explained how he thought democracy could be brought about in South Africa through nonviolent means. The prosecutor pointed to the Freedom Charter as proof that the ANC intended to overthrow the apartheid government by violence. Mandela explained patiently how the goals of the Freedom Charter could be achieved peacefully, step by step.

At the end of August, Prime Minister Verwoerd lifted the state of emergency. The defendants were now allowed to live at home during the remainder of the trial. Mandela was thankful to be able to sleep in his own bed, take a walk around the neighborhood if he felt like it, or stroll into a shop and buy a newspaper.

However, he had little time to relax and appreciate his freedom. From August to December, he worked so hard that he hardly saw his family. Mandela met with other ANC leaders—in secret, because it was now a serious crime just to belong to the ANC. He took on legal cases to make some money, using the Johannesburg apartment of Ahmed Kathrada as an office. And he traveled back and forth to the courthouse in Pretoria, where the trial was still proceeding.

157

Winnie was pregnant again, and in December 1960 she gave birth to another daughter, Zindziswa. Mandela missed this birth too, although not because of politics this time. His son Makgatho, who attended school in the Transkei, was ill, and Mandela drove all night to pick him up and bring him to Johannesburg for surgery.

As 1961 began, in Pretoria the prosecution gave its summation, and the defense gave its summation. Then the court adjourned to decide the verdict. It seemed likely that the judges would acquit the defendants. By this time, it was late in March.

During the adjournment, the ANC leaders met to discuss strategy. They thought that even if Nelson Mandela were found not guilty, the government would soon think up another reason to arrest him. They decided that Mandela should go underground, to promote and organize the ANC out of the government's view.

Mandela returned home, but only long enough to ask Winnie to pack a suitcase for him. "I'll be going away for a long time," he explained. If he were found guilty, he would be taken straight to prison. If he were found not guilty, he would take the opportunity to disappear. Mandela told his wife to be brave and strong and take good care of their children. Winnie said good-bye without a fuss, but tears ran down her face as she packed his clothes.

That afternoon Nelson Mandela picked up Makgatho and Makaziwe, his second son and his daughter from his marriage to Evelyn, at their mother's house in Orlando East. He took them for a ride in the countryside near Johannesburg. He would have taken his older son too, but Thembi was at school in the Transkei.

Mandela spent some hours with his children, walking on the veld and talking. Makgatho was only nine and Makaziwe seven, but Mandela guessed from their expressions that they knew something serious was happening.

Mandela's last public appearance was planned for March 25, at the All-In African Conference of ANC supporters in Pietermaritzburg, a town near Durban. The purpose of the conference was to demand a national convention to draw up a new constitution for South Africa. The ANC's position was that all the races of South Africa must be allowed to take part in the convention.

At the Indian meeting hall in Pietermaritzburg, the 1,400 delegates to the All-In African Conference were amazed and excited to see Nelson Mandela take the stage. He had not made a speech in public since 1952, when he was tried for "statutory communism." And although no one guessed it at the time, this would be his last public speech in South Africa for another twenty-nine years.

On March 29 the judges of the Treason Trial gave their verdict: not guilty. They explained that the government had failed to prove that the ANC was a communist organization. They had also failed to prove that Nelson Mandela and the other defendants had conspired to overthrow the government through violence.

The spectators rejoiced, singing the ANC anthem, "Nkosi Sikelel' iAfrika." They laughed, shed happy tears, and carried the victorious defense attorneys around on their shoulders. Mandela, stylish as usual in a checked suit, hugged Winnie.

But he did not return home, and he did not appear at a celebration that night at Bram Fischer's house. He was underground, staying at a "safe house," the apartment of a trusted friend in Johannesburg. The next day, he left on a trip to Port Elizabeth, Cape Town, and Durban.

For the next several months Mandela kept on the move from safe house to safe house, staying out of sight during the day and traveling mainly at night. He often disguised himself as a chauffeur, pretending to be driving his *baas*'s car. Besides changing from his suit into overalls and a chauffeur's cap, Mandela changed his manner. The police were looking for a bold, confident leader, but he acted the part of a passive, soft-voiced servant.

As for Prime Minister Verwoerd, he was extremely displeased with the judges' decision in the Treason Trial. In August 1961 he appointed a new minister of justice, John Vorster. Vorster was a former Nazi sympathizer, imprisoned during World War II for pro-German activities. With the prime minister's approval, Vorster intended to deal with "the threat of subversion and revolution," as he called the ANC, in his own way. His own way would include the use of torture when questioning prisoners.

In some ways Nelson Mandela enjoyed his life on the run, traveling in disguise, suddenly popping up in public, and then disappearing again. He got great satisfaction out of outwitting the apartheid government. Mandela also enjoyed spending time by himself, after his lack of privacy in prison and then his hectic months before the end of the Treason Trial. However, he missed Winnie and his children terribly. He managed to see Winnie now and then, although she never knew when that would be. She would hear a knock at her bedroom window very early in the morning, and Mandela would be there for an hour. Then he would vanish again.

Soon it became too dangerous for Mandela to come home at all, because the secret police were watching the house day and night. Instead of Mandela coming to their home, Winnie would get a telephone call telling her to be ready at a certain time. At the appointed time, a car would drive up to the house. Winnie would follow it in her car to a place where another car would pick her up and drive to meet still another car. And so on through ten cars, before she finally arrived at a safe house where Mandela was waiting.

On May 31, 1961, Prime Minister Verwoerd planned to proclaim South Africa a republic, officially exiting the British Commonwealth. The Dutch-heritage Afrikaners looked forward to it as a day of liberation. They had longed for independence ever since the British took over the country in 1902. At last, they felt, they would be free to run their nation as they saw fit.

The month before, the ANC had written Verwoerd demanding that the government call a national convention, open to delegates of every race. Otherwise, the

ANC would begin a nationwide multiracial strike, a work stoppage crippling to industry and commerce. The point would be that most of the people of South Africa were *not* liberated in the new republic.

Verwoerd did not answer the letter, but the government prepared as if for war. Army and police reserves were called out, and yellow police vans drove around black neighborhoods, announcing through speakers that any strikers would lose their jobs. Without proof of employment in their pass books, the strikers could then be forced out of the cities. Political meetings were outlawed, and helicopters with searchlights scanned black townships to pick out any gatherings of people.

Even so, on May 29 thousands of workers did go on strike, disrupting many factories and industries. But Nelson Mandela could see that this would not be the "knockout punch" to white supremacy that he had hoped, and he called off the strike. Mandela met with Walter Sisulu to decide what to do next. They agreed that nonviolent protests were not working against the Nationalist government.

There were long, heated arguments among the ANC leaders. Mandela and Sisulu, as well as Joe Slovo and other communists, pointed to the recent successes of the armed revolutionaries in Cuba and Algeria. But Chief Luthuli and many of the ANC's Indian allies were absolutely committed to protest by peaceful means.

Finally they reached a compromise: Those who believed in controlled violence would form a new branch of the ANC, called Umkhonto we Sizwe, or "Spear of the Nation," or MK. Mandela, Sisulu, and Slovo would lead this branch. They decided to begin with a program of sabotage, blowing up such targets as power stations, government buildings, and railways. They would make every effort to commit sabotage without taking any human life, so as to avoid turning public opinion against them.

In the midst of the ANC's preparation for a sabotage campaign, the news came in October 1961 that Chief Luthuli had received the Nobel Peace Prize. This was a rebuke to the Verwoerd government, which tried to portray Luthuli as a dangerous communist. But the prize also caused difficulty for the Spear of the Nation, which did not want to embarrass Luthuli through their violent actions. They decided to wait until December, after the Nobel awards ceremonies, to begin the sabotage.

In January 1962 Nelson Mandela secretly left South Africa and went on a tour to gather support for the ANC.

He began in Tanganyika (later part of Tanzania), which had become independent from Britain only the year before. At each stop, he paid a visit to the country's head of state and asked for help. He traveled from Tanganyika to Nigeria, and Nigeria to Ethiopia by way of Sudan.

As Mandela boarded a plane to fly from the Sudan to Ethiopia, he caught sight of the pilot—a black man. *How can a black man fly an airplane?* Mandela caught himself wondering nervously. Then he realized with a shock how deeply even he, a leader of the black liberation movement, had been affected by apartheid. According to apartheid doctrine, black Africans were so inferior that only a white man could qualify as a pilot.

Mandela was thrilled to be outside South Africa for the first time in his life. He was inspired by his visits to a whole string of independent African countries, including Egypt, Algeria, and Morocco. But wherever he went, he found that his rival black liberation organization, the blacks-only PAC, had been there before. The PAC had misinformed officials in every country that the ANC was a communist organization, dominated by whites. In spite of this, Mandela received some support for the ANC, but not as much as he hoped.

Along the way Mandela caught up with his friend and partner Oliver Tambo. Tambo had been working hard for the ANC ever since he fled South Africa in 1960. He had established ANC offices in several African countries and also in England. Mandela accompanied Tambo to London, meeting with people who might be able to help the ANC. He also took time to see sights, such as Westminster Abbey, that he had heard so much about during his British-style education.

The Spear of the Nation had planned, if the Verwoerd government did not respond to their sabotage campaign, to begin armed rebellion next. To prepare himself for guerrilla warfare, Mandela returned to Ethiopia for an extended military training program. However, after a few weeks Walter Sisulu urged him to return, since the ANC needed him more at home.

Mandela had been out of the country for six months. While he was gone, Winnie was harassed over and over by police searching their house, frightening the children with their loud voices. Sometimes they stopped by just to demand where Mandela was. Walter Sisulu was also harassed regularly. He had been arrested and released six times during Mandela's absence.

Meanwhile, the ANC's sabotage campaign had not been very effective. The government had reacted only by passing harsher laws. The Sabotage Act of 1962 defined "sabotage" so broadly that it included such acts as unlawful entry, or even just putting up a poster. The maximum penalty for sabotage was death.

These laws did not make the ANC planners any more cautious. They felt that they had a permanent safe house at Liliesleaf Farm in Rivonia, ten miles north of Johannesburg. Before his trip abroad, Mandela had spent many days in a cottage on the farm. Winnie and the children had joined him there for pleasant weekends. The ANC leaders often met at Liliesleaf, and they kept detailed records and documents in the cottage. Mandela and others in the ANC had little respect for the Special Branch, not realizing that the secret police had become much better at their jobs.

In August 1962, in spite of advice to lie low, Mandela made a trip to Durban. He wanted to explain a new ANC policy to Indian leaders there, as well as to Chief Luthuli. Mandela attended several meetings in the Durban area, and he even went to a large party where there could have been police informers. On August 5, Mandela began driving back toward Johannesburg. He was wearing his usual disguise and driving with a white friend, Cecil Williams, as if he were the chauffeur.

The police were waiting for them outside Pietermaritzburg. Mandela tried to give a false name, but the arresting sergeant said, "*Ag*, you're Nelson Mandela." As Mandela commented afterward, he had been so careless that it was a wonder he wasn't captured sooner.

Mandela was arrested and taken to Johannesburg Fort. Then he was transferred to Pretoria, where it would be harder for his friends and family to visit. However, Winnie managed to travel from Johannesburg to Pretoria twice a week, bringing Mandela clean clothes and tasty food.

In October, Mandela was tried on the charges of inciting workers to act illegally (that is, go on strike) and of leaving the country without a valid travel permit. He appeared in court with a dramatic flourish, wearing not his customary suit and tie, but the traditional leopard-skin *kaross* of a Xhosa chief. He caught sight of Winnie in the spectators' gallery, wearing a beaded headdress and a long embroidered Xhosa skirt, and he smiled. All Mandela's friends and family in the gallery jumped to their feet, saluting him with the ANC thumbs-up fist and shouting, *"Amandla!"* ("Power!").

Mandela, speaking for himself in court, turned his trial into a judgment on the apartheid government. He did not contest the fact that he was guilty as charged. But he announced that he did not consider himself legally or morally bound to obey laws made by a Parliament in which he had no representation. He did not bother to defend himself for breaking laws that he called "immoral, unjust, and intolerable." He warned what would happen if the government continued to try to control the black population with violence: The blacks would rise up against the whites in a bloody civil war.

Mandela's defiant speech, accusing the apartheid government of injustice, was barely mentioned in the South African press. But outside the country, his words gained him an international reputation. Western countries with a tradition of human rights, as well as the many newly independent nonwhite countries, paid attention.

In Pretoria, even the prosecuting attorney for the government was deeply impressed. Toward the end of the trial, the prosecutor visited Mandela in his cell. He admitted that he despised what he had to do, and he shook Mandela's hand.

On November 7, 1962, the judge sentenced Nelson Mandela to five years, which he began serving in Pretoria Local Prison. Meanwhile, a militant branch of the PAC began acting out just what Mandela had predicted in court: racial violence. The PAC militants decided to begin attacking whites, any whites, whether they supported the apartheid government or not. They believed that this violence would inspire all the blacks in South Africa to join in an armed rebellion and overwhelm the white government.

Several of these attacks did take place, terrifying the white population. However, Verwoerd's government moved swiftly to arrest PAC leaders and round up their supporters. The nationwide uprising the PAC had hoped for did not happen.

Instead, in May 1963 Parliament passed the General Law Amendment Act. This act allowed the police to arrest anyone without a warrant and hold them in prison indefinitely, in solitary confinement, without even charging them with a crime. The prisoners had no right to any contact with family or a lawyer, and they could be questioned over and over. "Questioning" or "interrogation" became code words for beating and torture.

The government was determined to crush the ANC as well as the PAC. In July the police raided the safe house at Liliesleaf Farm and captured Walter Sisulu and several other ANC leaders. The police also found a large stash of documents, some of them in Nelson Mandela's handwriting. These documents—letters, plans, maps—proved without a doubt that the ANC was conspiring to commit sabotage. Sabotage was punishable by hanging.

On October 9, Mandela, Sisulu, and the other defendants were taken to the Supreme Court in Pretoria to hear the charges against them. As Mandela walked into the courtroom, the spectators were shocked at his appearance. A year ago he had looked like a heroic Xhosa chief, healthy and powerfully muscled, with a leopard-skin *kaross* on his broad shoulders.

Now Mandela looked shriveled, painfully thin from months of prison food. Part of the time, he had been kept in solitary confinement. There were bags under his eyes, and his cheeks were hollow. He wore the only clothes a convicted black prisoner was allowed: shorts, a khaki shirt, and sandals. Still, he had a big smile for his friends and family in the gallery.

171

Mandela and his codefendants were deeply touched that a team of white attorneys, including Bram Fischer and George Bizos, were willing to defend them in court. White South Africans were hysterical over the threat of black rebellion. The media were full of the government's claims that the accused were obviously guilty, even before they were charged with any crimes. Anyone who dared to say a good word for them was in danger.

In the next few weeks, as the defendants and their lawyers worked to prepare their case, Mandela was convinced that he would receive the death sentence. He told his friends he would use the court to accuse the apartheid government, letting the world outside South Africa judge who was guilty. He planned to give a speech from the dock that would sum up his view of injustice in South Africa. He would express his ideals for the democratic, multiracial country that South Africa could become.

On April 20, 1964, Nelson Mandela gave his speech to the court. Winnie was in the gallery, and so was his mother, Nosekeni Fanny. As Mandela spoke in a slow, clear voice, the courtroom became absolutely silent.

He noted the "many years of tyranny, exploitation, and oppression of my people by the whites." He explained how the ANC had first believed that peaceful protests would show the whites that reforms must be made. He pointed out that the apartheid government had ignored the just demands of the black South Africans for a multiracial political system. They had responded to peaceful protests with violent repression.

Therefore, after careful consideration, Mandela and the other ANC leaders had decided to use sabotage. They hoped that blowing up railroads and power stations, thus hurting the businesses and industries of South Africa, would convince the whites in power to change their policies. They also hoped thereby to bring the plight of the blacks in South Africa to the attention of other countries, which might be able to influence the white government.

Mandela denied that the ANC was controlled by the Communist Party, as the apartheid government claimed. The ANC had worked with the communists only as far as their aims were the same—to remove white supremacy from South Africa. Unlike the communists, he said, the ANC had never been against a capitalist economic system.

The ANC's goal was for all races to achieve political rights, so that they could all benefit from the market system as whites had done so far. "Africans want a just share in the whole of South Africa," Mandela said. They wanted freedom from grinding poverty, and they wanted dignity.

Mandela spoke for three hours. At last he came to his conclusion, the words that his attorney Bram Fischer had begged him to leave out of the speech. Fischer feared that these final words amounted to an invitation to the judge to sentence him to death. Mandela spoke them anyway:

"I have cherished the ideal of a democratic and free society in which all persons will live together in harmony and with equal opportunities. It is an ideal which I hope to live for and to achieve. But . . . if it needs be, it is an ideal for which I am prepared to die."

For several moments after Mandela stopped speaking, there was only silence. Then his listeners let out a deep sigh. In the gallery, women began to cry.

CHAPTER 13
ROBBEN ISLAND

IN JUNE 1964, AT THE END OF THE TRIAL, THE JUDGE found Mandela, Sisulu, Kathrada, and most of the other defendants guilty as charged. They fully expected to be sentenced to death. But instead the judge sentenced them to life imprisonment.

Mandela wondered if the judge might have been influenced by the outcry from other countries against the trial. The United Nations Security Council had urged the South African government to end the trial and release the prisoners. In the United States, Great Britain, and European countries, there were mass demonstrations in support of the defendants. However, Prime Minister Verwoerd assured the South African Parliament that he was not at all influenced by the many telegrams he had received. In fact, he had thrown them in the trash.

On the night of June 12, Mandela, Sisulu, Kathrada, and their fellow prisoners were taken secretly, under heavy guard, from the cells at the courthouse to a military airport. From there they were flown the one thousand miles directly to Robben Island, a few miles off the coast from Cape Town. Once a prison for African chiefs who resisted the British invaders, the island had since been used as a leper colony, and during World War II it had been a military defense site. Now the Verwoerd government was again using it to punish political prisoners.

June is a winter month in the Southern Hemisphere, and bitterly cold, wet winds from the Atlantic Ocean swept over the island. The prisoners were issued short pants, a thin jersey, a canvas jacket, and shoes without socks. Even in this brutal place, the fine distinctions of apartheid laws were observed. Kathrada, the one Indian prisoner in the group, received long pants instead of shorts, and socks with his shoes.

Mandela and the others were housed in the new maximum-security prison for political prisoners. Three sides of the prison building were rows of cells, with a cement courtyard in the middle, and the fourth side was a high wall patrolled by guards with German shepherd dogs. Each prisoner was put in a damp concrete cell, seven by eight feet, with two-foot-thick walls, and given three threadbare blankets and a straw mat. Instead of a toilet, each cell had an iron bucket that had to be emptied and cleaned every day. The lid of the bucket held the prisoner's water for washing and shaving.

The guards at Robben Island were all white Afrikaners, and they shouted at the prisoners in Afrikaans. At five thirty a.m. it was *"Word wakker!"* ("Wake up!"). Breakfast was mealie-pap porridge. Then the guards would shout, *"Val in!"* ("Fall in!"), and the prisoners would stand outside their cells for inspection while the warder walked by.

During the day, the prisoners sat cross-legged in rows in the courtyard, where they pounded larger rocks into gravel. It was hard, tedious labor, but not vigorous enough to keep the men warm. Guards stood over them to make sure they did not talk to one another. At noon there was a break for lunch, which was a foul-smelling soup or boiled mealies (corn kernels).

After lunch, the prisoners worked again until four p.m. Then they were allowed half an hour to clean up, as best they could, in cold seawater. But at least the prisoners could sing and talk to one another while they washed off the grime of their day's work.

At four thirty, a nonpolitical prisoner from the other cell blocks arrived on the corridor with supper. He dished it out, and the prisoners took it back to their cells to eat. The supper was more mealie-pap porridge, sometimes with a vegetable, sometimes with a small, gristly piece of meat. The prison authorities claimed that the prisoners on Robben Island were fed a "balanced diet." Nelson Mandela wrote in his autobiography that "it was indeed balanced—between the unpalatable and the inedible."

At eight p.m., the warder would order them to go to sleep. If the prisoners tried to whisper to one another, he shouted, *"Stilte in die gang!"* ("Quiet in the corridor!") There was no lights-out, since a mesh-covered bulb in each cell burned twenty-four hours a day. But the prisoners were not allowed to read or write at night.

The place was grim enough to crush a prisoner's spirit, but Mandela and his friends were determined not to be crushed. From the beginning, they asserted their dignity in every way that they could. When the guards demanded that the prisoners address them as *"baas,"* they refused. When the overseers demanded that the prisoners produce a certain amount of gravel every day, instead they slowed their pace and produced less and less.

One morning, after several months of breaking rocks in the courtyard, Mandela and the other prisoners were driven in a truck to a lime quarry. They spent the day digging limestone from the rock with pick and shovel. The guards stood over them and shouted, *"Gaan aan!"* ("Go on!"), urging them to work harder. It was exhausting labor, but the prisoners were cheered by being outside in the fresh air.

The worst thing about the quarry was the glaring sunlight reflected from the white lime. Combined with the constant rock dust, the glare hurt the prisoners' eyes and made it hard for them to see. Mandela repeatedly made official requests, for himself and the other prisoners, for sunglasses. But they were not allowed to buy them for another three years.

Because Nelson Mandela was a lawyer and a spokesman for his group, he was often asked to stand up for other prisoners. He protested when prisoners were beaten by a guard, and he got one brutal guard removed from the island. After Mandela had been on Robben Island for a year and a half, the International Red Cross was allowed to visit the political prisoners. Mandela gave the Red Cross representative a long list of complaints, including a request for long pants. The prison authorities ignored most of the complaints, but Mandela and his friends did at last receive long pants.

Backbreaking work, bad food, and lack of decent clothing were hard to bear, but other restrictions seemed even harsher to Mandela. The political prisoners were forbidden any news of the outside world—no newspapers, no radios. They were allowed to receive only one letter every six months. If that one letter did arrive, it was heavily censored. The censor cut out the disapproved sentences and paragraphs with razors, turning a long-awaited letter into a frustrating paper doily.

Mandela was also allowed only one visitor every six months, for half an hour. The first time Winnie visited, it was almost more painful than not seeing her. The prisoner had to sit in a cubicle on one side of a wall, while the visitor sat in a facing cubicle on the other side of the wall. They saw each other through a small, thick glass window drilled with a few holes to permit conversation. They had to speak English, not Xhosa, so the guards could understand them.

Winnie was dressed up for the visit and looked more beautiful than ever to Mandela, but he could see that she was under a strain. Guards on both sides of the wall stood right behind each of them, watching and listening. It was forbidden to talk about anything other than family matters. If either Winnie or Mandela said anything even slightly political, their precious time together could be cut off.

Winnie could not tell Mandela about the hardships she was suffering. She was banned to Johannesburg and forbidden to attend meetings or social gatherings. The police raided her house. She trusted a man who turned out to be a secret police informer.

Worse was to come the next year, in 1965. Winnie was banned even more tightly, restricted to such a small area that she had to give up her job as a social worker. She loved that job, and it was her only source of income. She tried to find other jobs, but the security police bullied the new employers into firing her. They even forced Zeni's and Zindzi's schools to expel them. And they continued to harass Winnie by raiding her house.

Mandela and the other political prisoners on Robben Island were allowed to study, although there were many obstacles. They could not study politics or military history. When they tried to buy books or borrow them from a public library, there were long waits, or they might never get the books.

Many of the prisoners, including Mandela, needed reading glasses, but at first they were not allowed to have the glasses. They were also not permitted to have anything like a desk or a chair. After many months of complaints, the authorities allowed each prisoner a board, attached to the wall of his cell, to write on, and a stool to sit on.

One of the subjects Mandela studied seriously was the Afrikaans language. Some of his fellow prisoners could not understand why he wanted to learn the language of their oppressors. Mandela explained that it would give him greater insight into the minds of the Afrikaners. Knowing their language would help him deal with the guards and officials on Robben Island, and after prison it would help him deal with the Afrikaners in power. (Mandela refused to believe, in spite of their life sentences, that he and his friends would die in prison.)

The prisoners craved news of the outside world, but the prison authorities were determined not to let the political prisoners have it. However, Mandela and his friends were even more determined to get the news. Noticing that their guards at the quarry had sandwiches wrapped in newspaper, the prisoners would secretly pluck these pieces of paper from the trash, hide them under their shirts, and read them later in their cells. They would share their precious scraps of news carefully, because possessing a newspaper was a serious violation of the prison rules.

One afternoon, returning from a day of labor, Mandela spotted a whole newspaper lying on a bench in the corridor. There was no one in sight. Mandela grabbed the paper, smuggled it into his cell, and began to read it like a starving man wolfing down food. While he was reading, a prison officer and two guards showed up and caught him with the goods. His punishment for breaking this rule was three days in solitary confinement, with no meals except for rice water.

For Nelson Mandela, solitary confinement was harder to bear than the lack of food. There was nothing to do, nothing to see except the four walls of the cell, and worst of all, no one to talk to. He lost track of time, and his mind began to play tricks on him. He was glad if a cockroach crawled out of a crack, because even an insect was some kind of company.

Although the rules on Robben Island were so harsh, the prisoners could sometimes get around them with the help of a friendly warder. The warders were poorly paid, so they could be bribed with cigarettes or a small amount of money. Sometimes they simply responded to friendly treatment from a prisoner. Mandela's policy was to treat each warder as if he was a decent human being, and he often succeeded in getting decent treatment in return.

In 1966 Mandela heard that Prime Minister Verwoerd was dead. Ironically, he had been stabbed to death not by any of the black people he had oppressed, but by a mentally unbalanced white messenger. Some prisoners thought Verwoerd's death was good news, but the new prime minister, John Vorster, continued the same apartheid policies. The Terrorism Act of 1967 gave the secret police even more leeway. On Robben Island, the decent warder who oversaw the quarry was replaced with a warder known for his brutal treatment of prisoners.

When Mandela first began serving his sentence on the island, he and his supporters were hopeful that he might be released within a few years. There had been so much criticism of his trial, both within South Africa and internationally, that it seemed the government would have to pay attention and eventually let him go. But the years on the tiny, bleak island dragged on. The government banned any publication of Mandela's words or photos of him, and gradually the public seemed to forget about him.

In 1968 Mandela's sister Mabel brought their mother to Robben Island for a visit. Mandela was alarmed to see how old and frail Nosekeni Fanny had grown, and he worried that he might never see her again. In fact, several weeks later she died of a heart attack. Mandela asked the authorities for permission to attend his mother's funeral in the Transkei, but it was denied. Among the Thembu, the tradition was that a parent would be buried by the eldest son, and it hurt Mandela that he could not even do that for his mother.

In July of the next year, Nelson Mandela was hit with a harder blow: His older son, Thembi, twenty-four years old, died in a car accident. Mandela asked permission to attend his son's funeral, but again permission was denied. Thembi's death was especially bitter because the boy had never forgiven Mandela for divorcing his mother, Evelyn. Although Thembi lived in nearby Cape Town, only a few miles from Robben Island, he had not visited his father in prison.

A few weeks before Thembi's death, Winnie Mandela had been arrested. The police dragged her out of the house as Zeni, only ten years old, and Zindzi, eight, clung to her. She was held in solitary confinement for over a year.

Officially, the prison authorities did not allow the prisoners to see news items. But when there was bad news about Winnie, they deliberately tormented Mandela by leaving news clippings where he could find them. Mandela suffered not only for his wife but also for his two young daughters.

Zeni and Zindzi were now in boarding school in Swaziland, a small kingdom on the eastern border of South Africa. There they could get a decent education without harassment from the secret police. But with their mother and father both in prison, they would not be able to come home during vacations. Instead they stayed with family friends in Johannesburg. They were not allowed to visit their father until they were sixteen.

Mandela kept in touch with his children as well as he could through letters. "My darlings," he wrote Zeni and Zindzi. "Once again our beloved Mummy has been arrested and now she and Daddy are away in jail." Although Mandela's daughters were so young, he asked them to believe that their sacrifice was necessary, and that they would understand when they were older.

186

Mandela felt helpless to protect his family, and he knew he was growing out of touch with them. Over and over he dreamed the same nightmare: He was released from prison and returned to Johannesburg. He walked miles and miles through the eerily lifeless city. When he reached his home in Orlando, all the doors and windows were open, and his house was empty. There was no clue as to where his wife and daughters had gone.

Mandela and his friends labored in the lime quarry on Robben Island for thirteen years. However, in 1973 a new commanding officer took over the prison, and conditions improved somewhat. The prisoners were not forced to work so hard, and they had time to carry on lengthy discussions. They even divided into study groups and lectured one another on various subjects during the day. With more opportunity to study, several men received advanced degrees. They nicknamed Robben Island "the University."

The better-educated prisoners were eager to share their knowledge with the others, and they started a literacy program for the inmates who had never learned to read or write. They even encouraged their warders to improve themselves by taking courses in their free time.

Continuing their education was one of the ways that Mandela and the others kept their sanity, as year after year went by. Another important link to mental health, for Mandela, was his fitness routine. Every morning he woke up even before the warder shouted down the hall. Four days a week, he ran in place in his cell for over half an hour. He also did push-ups, sit-ups, and deep knee bends.

A cherished part of Mandela's private routine was imagining time with his beloved wife. Every morning he carefully dusted his photo of Winnie. He touched his nose to hers, as he used to do before his imprisonment. In the evenings he wrote her long letters, remembering scenes from their life together and describing a road trip they would take when he was finally released.

By the late 1970s the prisoners were no longer forced to do manual labor. Mandela seized the chance to start his own vegetable garden. The little patch of ground he was allowed was stony and dry, but he welcomed the challenge. As he cultivated his tomatoes and chilies, he remembered fondly his years at Clarkebury, working in Reverend Harris's garden. His crops improved year by year, and he shared the produce with the warders as well as with his fellow prisoners.

• • •

In 1977 Mandela's daughter Zeni married a prince of Swaziland. Mandela worried that she was too young, at eighteen, to get married. He was not allowed to attend her wedding, so he asked his friend and attorney George Bizos to stand in for him.

Once Zeni had married into the royal family of Swaziland, she was allowed special diplomatic privileges. The next year she and her husband and their baby were able to visit Mandela on Robben Island in a room without barriers. For the first time since 1964, Mandela was permitted to hug his daughter. He felt almost dizzy. He took the newborn baby in his work-roughened hands and held her for the rest of the visit. It was traditional for the grandfather to name a baby, and Mandela chose the name Zaziwe ("hope").

CHAPTER 14
FREE MANDELA

WHEN NELSON MANDELA WAS FIRST TRIED FOR treason in 1962, black people's lives under the apartheid system seemed as bad as they could get. But in the following years, the plight of black South Africans grew steadily worse. In the cities almost one hundred thousand Africans were pushed out, as one by one the "black spots" were erased. Southwest of Johannesburg, a whole group of townships was created to house the thousands of blacks evicted from the city. This area was called Soweto, standing for South Western Townships.

Blacks were also forced out of their homes in parts of the countryside where whites lived and farmed. The population of the already overcrowded "Bantu homelands" doubled. More than ever, low-paid migrant labor for white-owned farms and industries was the only way of life open to black men.

NELSONMANDELA

Mandela was sad and angry that his old friend and cousin Kaiser Matanzima was cooperating with the Bantustan plan for the Transkei. Matanzima went along with the government's line that black South Africans would be better off as citizens of their supposedly independent tribal homelands, developing separately from white South Africa. In return, the government allowed Matanzima to become dictator of the Transkei. At least Evelyn, Mandela's first wife, benefitted from this outcome. Matanzima helped her to acquire a trading store, formerly owned by whites, near Queenstown.

In KwaZulu, the Zulu tribal area, Chief Mangosuthu Buthelezi likewise ruled. However, Buthelezi managed to have it both ways. He refused to accept the government's plan to separate the "Bantu homelands" from South Africa. He built up his Inkatha Freedom Party. He demanded that the government ban on the ANC be lifted, and that political prisoners, especially Nelson Mandela, be freed.

During the 1970s the black consciousness movement sprang up in South Africa, led by a medical student named Steve Biko. Black consciousness urged Africans to cultivate black pride and black achievement, rejecting control by whites or even any white help. The system of "Bantu

191

education," under which black South Africans received only enough education to become migrant workers or servants, was especially scorned.

In June 1976 mass protests broke out because the government had ordered the Bantu schools to teach courses in the hated Afrikaans language. At a peaceful march of ten thousand in Soweto, the police fired on the unarmed young people, killing one boy. The demonstrators rioted, and more riots and demonstrations erupted across the country as the news spread. By 1977, almost six hundred people had died. Later that year, Steve Biko was imprisoned, tortured, and beaten to death, and another wave of riots broke out.

The government tried to control the black consciousness protests by arresting the leaders, and a new wave of political prisoners arrived on Robben Island. These younger men were determined not to cooperate with the prison authorities in any way or to associate with anyone except other blacks. At first they were scornful of Nelson Mandela, Walter Sisulu, and their friends. Mandela was surprised and indignant that the new prisoners considered him a "moderate"—maybe even a sellout.

Gradually, however, Mandela brought most of the young

men around to his point of view. They saw that although he was courteous and even friendly with the white guards, he kept his dignity and self-respect. They realized that it worked better to make requests of the prison authorities over and over, politely but firmly, than it did to shout and swear at them. They came to understand that the prison was a small-scale model of the apartheid system outside. On Robben Island, Mandela and his friends were perfecting their self-control, persistence, and cunning. With these same techniques, they planned to bring down apartheid in South Africa.

Meanwhile, in 1976 Nelson Mandela was given a chance to leave Robben Island. Jimmy Kruger, the minister of prisons, visited Mandela and made him an offer. If Mandela was willing to move to the Transkei, the Bantustan where Kaiser Matanzima ruled, he could go free. Of course, that would mean giving up any claim to South African citizenship. Mandela turned the offer down.

During the 1980s, the mood of the white population in South Africa toward apartheid began to change. Foreign investors, fearing that civil war could break out in South Africa, withdrew their money, and this hurt South African businesses. The United States and many European nations, as well as other members of the United Nations, restricted trade with South Africa. The price of oil, which South Africa had to import, shot up.

South African businesses were hurt in other ways by apartheid policies. Because of technological advances, farms and industries no longer wanted only the low-skilled migrant laborers produced by "Bantu education." They needed skilled black workers, and the economy was suffering from the lack of them.

At the same time, after many years of public silence about Nelson Mandela, a campaign sprang up. FREE MANDELA! First it was a headline, early in 1980, on a black newspaper in Soweto. Then the slogan appeared on posters or in letters painted on the walls of buildings.

In March, on the eve of the twentieth anniversary of the Sharpeville massacre, a huge rally for Mandela's release took place at the University of the Witwatersrand. Zindzi Mandela, nineteen, gave a speech reminding the crowd that her father had once offered a way toward a peaceful multiracial South Africa. "The call for Mandela's release is merely to say there is an alternative to the inevitable bloodbath."

The international pressure on South Africa to "Free Mandela!" grew and grew. Nelson Mandela became a world-famous symbol of resistance to apartheid. In New York, the Security Council of the United Nations voted to ban weapons sales to South Africa. In California, a college student named Barack Obama was inspired by Mandela's example. At a rally to persuade Occidental College to withdraw its investments in South Africa, Obama gave his first political speech.

The South African government, now headed by Prime Minister P. W. Botha (nicknamed "the Great Crocodile"), announced publicly that Nelson Mandela would never be released. Privately, the government wondered what to do with him. The minister of justice, Kobie Coetsee, pondered a report from the prison authorities on Mandela's character.

The report noted, in a baffled way, that Mandela gave the *impression* of good behavior. He worked politely, in a friendly manner, but tirelessly to get what he wanted from the prison system. He was remarkably self-disciplined. In other words, he had become a truly effective "trouble-maker."

Imprisonment had not broken Mandela's idealism or

his determination to achieve political liberation for black South Africans. He had deep confidence that this was his mission in life. However, he was practical, willing to work out reasonable ways to reach his goals. In short, the report summarized, he had the potential to be "the number one black leader in South Africa."

The government still did not know what to do with Mandela, but they did decide to move him off Robben Island. They hoped that this would help them avoid some of the bad publicity they were getting and also break up the close-knit group of political prisoners on the island. At the end of March 1982, Mandela—along with Walter Sisulu, Ahmed Kathrada, and a few others—was transferred to Pollsmoor Prison on the mainland.

It was wrenching for Mandela and the others to leave the community they had built over the years, but the conditions at Pollsmoor, a few miles from Cape Town, seemed luxurious. The cells had real beds with sheets, instead of mats on stone floors; indoor toilets instead of buckets; and dinners with meat and vegetables. Even better, the prisoners were allowed to read US and British newspapers and magazines. When Winnie and others in Mandela's family visited, the visiting room was more humane, and the guard was courteous.

In March 1984 Winnie came for a visit with a big difference. Instead of having to talk to his wife through a wall of glass, Mandela found himself with her in a room without any barriers. For the first time in twenty-one years, he was allowed to touch his wife. He had dreamed about this moment for so long that he could hardly believe he was holding her close.

Outside in South Africa, the ANC had become a strong organization once more, and they began a new campaign of strikes, boycotts, and sabotage. Also, the ANC now had help from African countries bordering South Africa. Botswana, Mozambique, and Zimbabwe (formerly Rhodesia) were all independent nations sympathetic to the black liberation struggle in South Africa. Violence between black and white was growing, and there was real danger that civil war would tear the country apart.

P. W. Botha, now holding the new office of state president, was all in favor of white supremacy, but he was not a fanatic like Verwoerd or Vorster. He publicly announced that apartheid could not be maintained, and he made some small reforms. The WHITES ONLY signs on public facilities such as parks and swimming pools began to disappear, and there was talk about repealing the laws against interracial marriage. (Mandela later remarked wryly, "It is not my ambition to marry a white woman or swim in a white pool. It is political equality that we want.")

However, Botha wanted to control the ANC without making any important concessions to it. In January 1985 he made a speech offering Nelson Mandela freedom if he "unconditionally rejected violence as a political instrument." It was clear to Mandela that the government was trying to separate him from the ANC. Still, he took the opportunity to make his own point.

In reply to Botha, Mandela wrote a speech that Zindzi gave for him in February. The audience was a rally at the Jabulani Stadium in Soweto. They were celebrating the Nobel Peace Prize received by Bishop Desmond Tutu of Cape Town, a black antiapartheid activist. Zindzi read her father's speech in a clear, passionate voice.

If President Botha wanted peace, said Mandela, "let him renounce violence." The ANC had made peaceful requests and protests for decades, only to be ignored by the apartheid government or harshly repressed. As for freedom, what kind of freedom would Mandela have, even outside prison, when he could not vote in his own country? At the end of the speech, the enormous multiracial crowd in the stadium burst into cheers and chants.

In Europe and the United States, the antiapartheid movement continued to grow. The movement was especially strong in Great Britain, with its close connection with South Africa. In 1984 a band called the Special AKA released a song, "Free Nelson Mandela," which hit the top ten on the pop music charts in the UK. The next year a musicians' protest group, Artists United Against Apartheid, raised one million dollars for the ANC in exile.

For the next few years, the white government of South Africa made cautious, stop-and-start moves toward negotiating with the ANC through Mandela. Foreign visitors met with Mandela, trying to mediate an agreement between the ANC and the apartheid government. Mandela explained to them that he was committed to a multiracial South Africa; he did not want to drive whites out of the country. As the Freedom Charter of 1955 declared, "South Africa belongs to all who live in it, black and white." But South Africa must become a democracy, with full participation by all racial groups.

The violence in the country grew, and many black leaders were confident that they would overturn the white government by force. The government responded with more repression. They also encouraged fighting between Chief Buthelezi's Zulu Inkatha Freedom Party and the ANC, even supplying the Zulus with training and weapons.

In May 1986 President Botha ordered air strikes on three cities in Botswana, Zambia, and Zimbabwe, accusing them of harboring ANC terrorists. He declared a state of emergency in South Africa, making any criticism of the government illegal. Thousands of antiapartheid activists were thrown into prison.

In spite of the growing spiral of violence and repression and more violence, Nelson Mandela hoped to work out a deal between the ANC and the government. He talked at length with Kobie Coetsee, the minister of prisons, and then with a secret committee representing the white government. The man Mandela really wanted to sit down with, the one who had the power to actually *make* a deal, was President Botha. But Botha still did not want to negotiate.

At the end of 1988 Mandela alone was moved to an even more comfortable prison, the Victor Verster prison farm. He was kept in a private house with gardens and a swimming pool. By now the government was worried about his health, and they had a doctor examine him every day.

Mandela enjoyed his new privileges, but he stuck to the discipline that had held him together for so many years. He rose early, he exercised, and he made his own bed, although he now had a household staff. He continued to study, and he finally passed his law degree.

Finally a meeting between Mandela and Botha was arranged for July 5, 1989. Mandela was allowed a new suit, shirt, tie, and shoes for the occasion. The prison commander himself tied Mandela's tie for him in a Windsor knot. With great secrecy, Mandela was driven to the president's official residence in Cape Town. Mandela did not know what to expect from Botha, and he had heard that the other man had a terrible temper.

But when Mandela walked into the president's office, Botha walked forward to meet him halfway, smiling and with hand outstretched. Tea was served, and the two men chatted about South African history. Nothing was settled—except that clearly, the white government had accepted Nelson Mandela as the man to negotiate with.

About a month later, President Botha resigned and F. W. de Klerk took over as head of the government of South Africa. De Klerk had always supported apartheid in the past, but he was a practical man. He recognized that the whites in South Africa would have to begin sharing political power with the other racial groups, and he intended to resolve the conflict peacefully. In September 1989, when Desmond Tutu, now an archbishop, led a march in Cape Town protesting police brutality, de Klerk showed that he had meant what he said. The nonviolent march was allowed to take place.

President de Klerk continued his program of reforms. In the fall of 1989 he released several political prisoners, including Walter Sisulu and Ahmed Kathrada. Furthermore, they were allowed to carry on ANC activities, as long as they were nonviolent. In December, Mandela was taken to meet with de Klerk for the first time. Mandela was deeply impressed that de Klerk was actually listening to him, trying to understand his position. Afterward he reported to other ANC leaders, "Mr. de Klerk is a man we can do business with."

On February 11, 1990, Nelson Mandela was released from prison. For the first time in more than twenty-seven years, he was a free man. Newspapers and TV around the world showed him walking out the front gate of his prison, holding Winnie's hand. The public had not even seen a picture of him since he entered prison in 1962 as a black-haired, burly man of forty-four.

What they saw now was a gray-haired man of seventy-one with not much flesh on his tall frame. His smile was as radiant as ever, and a serene spirit shone through. It seemed that the fiery freedom fighter had been transformed into a kindly grandfather.

At the city hall in Cape Town, ten thousand people had waited for hours to see this man. Mandela understood that it was important to show them that he had not sold out to the apartheid government. Stepping out on the balcony, he raised his fist in the ANC salute. *"Amandla!"* ("Power!") he shouted, and the crowd roared back, *"Ngawethu!"* ("The power is ours!")

Soon after his release, Mandela began traveling abroad. He wanted to gather international support for the ANC and to urge other nations to keep trade sanctions on South Africa until apartheid was ended. Besides, after so many years in a prison cell, he was eager to see the world. Beginning with a tour of independent African nations, he then flew to Sweden, where Oliver Tambo was living in exile, and on to London.

A second trip took Mandela to other countries in Europe, where he was welcomed by the heads of state. In the United States, he was given a ticker-tape parade in New York City. He addressed the US Congress in Washington DC.

During the next few years, Nelson Mandela and the ANC continued to negotiate with the white government. By 1993 they had agreed on a transitional government, leading up to national elections in 1994. For their work in avoiding a bloody civil war in South Africa, Mandela and de Klerk were awarded a joint Nobel Peace Prize.

Even so, during the years between Mandela's release from prison and the first democratic elections, South Africa teetered on the edge of civil war. Hard-line Afrikaners were bitterly disappointed in de Klerk's turn away from apartheid. They demanded their own independent white state, separate from South Africa.

In April 1993 a popular black leader, Chris Hani, was assassinated by a member of a white supremacist group. The black population was on the point of erupting in violent revenge. Immediately Mandela went on TV to plead for peace.

"Tonight," Mandela said, "I am reaching out to every single South African, black and white, from the very depths of my being." He pointed out that the assassin had been Polish, not South African, and that a white Afrikaner neighbor of Hani's had called the police to the scene of the crime. "Now is the time for all South Africans to stand together against those who, from any quarter, wish to destroy what Chris Hani gave his life for—the freedom of all of us."

Mandela's leadership helped prevent civil war from breaking out, but the violence of blacks against blacks continued without letup. The years of apartheid's "Bantu education" had produced a whole generation of angry, unemployed black youth, and they often took out their frustrations against one another. In the townships and squatter camps around Johannesburg, as well as in KwaZulu, Inkatha Freedom Party supporters battled ANC supporters. The slaughter was horrific, and politicians had little control.

Meanwhile, sadly, Mandela's family life was not what he had dreamed of during his long years in prison. He came to realize that Winnie no longer loved him, and that they did not even agree politically. She had become much more militant than Mandela, often urging violence and revenge in her speeches. In 1992 they separated, finally divorcing in 1996.

Just as painful, most of Mandela's children were not close to him and had not turned out the way he hoped. Thembi had died while Mandela was on Robben Island; Makgatho had been expelled from school and had never completed his studies. Makaziwe had refused to pursue a college education, as her father wished, and now she was divorced with two children. Zindzi and Zeni were on better terms with Mandela, but Zindzi had had children by two different men. The second one had beaten her so badly that she almost died.

"When your life is the struggle, as mine was," Mandela wrote in his autobiography, "there is little room left for family." To become "father of the nation," as he was called, he had to give up being the father of his own family. Zindzi joked bitterly that at least while he was in prison, she was allowed to visit him twice a month. After her father was released, he often didn't have time to see her.

CHAPTER 15

PRESIDENT MADIBA

ON APRIL 27, 1994, BLACK AS WELL AS WHITE SOUTH Africans went to the polls to vote. It was a joyous day, and yet Nelson Mandela felt somber, too. He thought of his friends who had not lived to see this day: Bram Fischer, Oliver Tambo, Albert Luthuli. He laid a wreath on the grave of the founding president of the ANC, John Dube, and then went to cast his own vote in a country schoolhouse.

All over South Africa, citizens stood in long lines outside polling places, sometimes waiting for hours. Blacks felt that by voting, their dignity had at last been restored. Many whites felt, with great relief, that the burden of apartheid had been lifted from them, too.

When the ballots were counted, Nelson Mandela's ANC party had won by more than 62 percent. De Klerk's

National Party had received just over 20 percent of the vote, and the Zulu Inkatha Freedom Party just over 10 percent.

On May 10, 1994, Nelson Mandela was inaugurated as the first black president of South Africa. The whole world celebrated with South Africa. One hundred seventy countries sent representatives to Pretoria to honor the occasion.

The new national flag, combining the ANC colors of black, green, and yellow with the Afrikaner and British colors of red, white, and blue, was raised. Two national anthems were played: "Nkosi Sikelel' iAfrika," the ANC anthem, and "Die Stem van Suid-Afrika," the Afrikaner anthem. At the same time, military jet planes roared overhead in close formation—the same jets that had been bought to fight the black liberation movement. In his inauguration speech, President Mandela pledged to help "build the society in which all South Africans, both black and white, will be able to walk tall . . . a rainbow nation at peace with itself and the world."

At the age of seventy-five, Nelson Mandela found himself chief of a huge, needy, quarrelsome tribe. He was well aware that in several other African nations, such as Kenya and Zimbabwe, civil war between rival tribes had disrupted the newly independent countries. Ghana had been afflicted by military takeovers.

So Mandela's mission, as he saw it, was to get the bitterest enemies to cooperate in the new South Africa. It would be hard, frustrating, thankless work, but he had the self-discipline and patience that he had perfected during twenty-seven years in prison. He also applied the lessons he had learned as a boy, watching Regent Jongintaba moderate the Thembu councils with the principle of *ubuntu*.

In appointing his new cabinet, Mandela included people who had opposed him as well as his political friends. F. W. de Klerk, head of the opposing National Party, became one deputy president, while Thabo Mbeki, who had devoted his life to the ANC in exile, became the other. Kobie Coetsee, the former prisons minister, became president of the senate; Joe Slovo, former leader of the South African Communist Party, became minister of housing. Zulu chief Mangosuthu Buthelezi, leader of the Inkatha Freedom Party, was appointed minister of home affairs. Dullah Omar, ethnically Indian and legal adviser to antiapartheid activists, became minister of justice.

In a surprise move, Mandela kept the white secretaries and servants from de Klerk's staff. He charmed them all, shaking their hands and remembering their names. In turn, they called him "Madiba," his clan name. Even his white Afrikaner bodyguards quickly became devoted to the first black president of South Africa. "I'd take the bullet for him," said one bodyguard.

Mandela went to some lengths to reassure the white business leaders that he intended to work with them. South Africa was highly industrialized, and its economy could not function without technicians, business managers, and professionals. But apartheid policies had stunted black education for so long that if the whites fled, there would not be enough black technicians, business managers, and professionals to take their places.

To prevent whites from leaving the country, Mandela had to convince them that they were safe and welcome in the new South Africa. One impressive gesture he made was to invite Percy Yutar, the attorney who had argued for the death sentence for Mandela in 1964, to lunch. Yutar, overwhelmed, called Mandela "this saintly man."

To show his all-inclusive South African patriotism, Mandela publicly supported the national rugby team, the Springboks. The black people of South Africa had always considered rugby as the sport of the white oppressors, especially of the Afrikaners. But in the 1995 World Cup final, when against the odds the Springboks defeated New Zealand, President Mandela walked onto the field wearing a green Springbok jersey. As he presented the captain with the trophy, the white crowd in the stadium chanted their approval: "Nel-son! Nel-son!"

On the other hand, Mandela needed to reassure the black population that reforms were coming. The black masses were desperate. Blacks had suffered from widespread unemployment since the 1980s, and almost half of the families in South Africa lived below the poverty line. One-third of the population could not read or write. Mandela's administration launched a program of free health care for pregnant women and small children, and free meals for primary school children, but many of the needed reforms would take time.

As president of South Africa, Mandela continued

to live in the disciplined way he had lived—and maintained his health and sanity—in prison. He awoke at four thirty a.m., made his own bed, went for a long walk, and read the newspapers before breakfast. However, he gave careful thought to the clothes he wore. Since Mandela was a little boy, he had understood that style was important.

Style was not just on the surface; it could be an expression of deep values. When Gadla Henry gave young Rolihlahla his first pair of pants to wear to school, he showed respect for the Western education that his son was undertaking. When the prisoner Mandela strode into the courtroom at the Treason Trial wearing the *kaross* of a Xhosa chief, he showed his defiant pride in his tribal heritage. As president of South Africa, Mandela frequently appeared in a colorful flowered silk shirt instead of a suit. He explained that the bright, relaxed shirts made him *feel* his freedom, after twenty-seven years in prison.

President Mandela was comfortable and friendly with humble people, but he was also at ease with royalty. When Queen Elizabeth II of Great Britain arrived for a state visit, the two clearly enjoyed each other's company. The queen had been sympathetic to the striving of black

South Africans during Mandela's prison years. Although Mandela told her, "I'm only a country boy," he had the natural dignity of a fellow ruler.

While Mandela was still on Robben Island, he had managed to write a good part of his autobiography. He now went back to this project, with the help of writer Richard Stengel, and completed the book. In 1994, it was finally published as *Long Walk to Freedom*. The book was translated into many languages, even Afrikaans.

At home and abroad, Nelson Mandela won many friends with his gestures of goodwill and forgiveness. However, he felt there also had to be some kind of public acknowledgment of the nation's bitter past. In 1996 he launched the Truth and Reconciliation Commission, with Archbishop Desmond Tutu as chairman. The idea of this project was to encourage people who had committed political crimes under the apartheid regime to admit their guilt. If they did so, they would not be tried and punished as criminals.

During more than two years of testimony by both victims and perpetrators, many horrifying crimes were laid bare. Most of them had been committed by the apartheid regime, but the ANC and Inkatha had also been guilty of torture and assassinations. From the apartheid government, the most impressive witness was Pik Botha, former foreign minister under Prime Minister Vorster. He admitted that he, as well as the rest of Vorster's cabinet, had been fairly sure that the police were torturing and killing political prisoners. But he had done nothing about it.

Forty years of apartheid could not be undone in the five-year term of Mandela's presidency, and by 1999 there were still grave problems facing South Africa. A frightening crime wave swept the country, and the police, trained for so long to persecute political enemies, were not able to handle it. The white population complained about crime, political corruption, and losing their former privileges. In spite of Mandela's reassurances, many white doctors, accountants, and computer experts left for other countries. Among blacks, while some moved into the middle class or even became rich, the vast majority remained in poverty.

But President Madiba had done as much as he could. Although he was surprisingly healthy for his age of eighty, he had no intention of running for re-election in 1999. He backed Thabo Mbeki, son of his fellow prisoner

Govan Mbeki, as the ANC candidate for president. As deputy president, Mbeki had already taken on much of the administrative work, while Mandela was the public face of South Africa.

In Mandela's farewell speech to Parliament on March 29, 1999, he said, "The long walk continues."

CHAPTER 16

FATHER OF HIS COUNTRY

ON HIS EIGHTIETH BIRTHDAY, IN JULY 1998, NELSON Mandela married for the third time. His new wife was Graça Machel, widow of the former president of Mozambique, Samora Machel. Machel was a steady, compassionate woman, and she was accustomed to public life. They shared a strong interest in children's welfare, and together they raised money for children's aid organizations.

Mandela always claimed he was a country boy at heart, and after leaving the presidency he moved to the house he had built in Qunu. Mandela's spacious one-story redbrick house was set on a hillside and shielded by a wall and shrubs. The village in the Transkei had not changed much since the years when Rolihlahla was growing up. Here he could relax and take early morning walks over the hills. Knowing how important his own education had been to him, a child of a poor family, he helped raise funds for a new schoolhouse in Qunu.

However, Mandela was not content to take it easy in the countryside for long. He also spent time in Johannesburg, where he worked with the Nelson Mandela Foundation. The purpose of this organization was to combat AIDS, and to fund rural development and school construction.

Although Mandela had left the presidency, he still played a public role in international politics. He traveled abroad, to the United States and European countries, to encourage economic investment in South Africa. He continued to meet with world leaders, including US president George W. Bush, who awarded him the Presidential Medal of Freedom.

As when Mandela was president, he urged other nations to settle conflicts by peaceful means. He felt that others, especially other African nations, should learn from the way South Africa had been able to negotiate its conflicts, despite the history of injustice and violence. He had been greatly troubled by the civil wars in Rwanda and the

Democratic Republic of the Congo, and also by the failure of democracy in Nigeria.

In 2003, when US President George W. Bush and UK prime minister Tony Blair prepared to launch a war against Iraq, Mandela called the war "a tragedy." He criticized Bush and Blair for undermining the United Nations, which had not yet completed an investigation of Iraq's weapons. And Mandela accused Bush personally of using the war to get control of Iraqi oil.

Meanwhile, South Africa under the new president, Thabo Mbeki, still faced the same problems as under Mandela: massive unemployment and runaway crime. The country was also suffering an epidemic of the disease HIV/AIDS. Before Mandela left office, a government plan to fight AIDS had been launched. But then Mbeki changed his mind and declared that AIDS was the result of poverty, rather than a retrovirus.

For the next four years, the government refused to provide antiretroviral medicine to the victims of AIDS, even to prevent the transfer of AIDS from pregnant women to their babies. Mbeki also accused white campaigners against AIDS of racism. Mandela was dismayed. Mbeki's change in policy would end up costing the lives of hundreds of thousands of South Africans, and it would help to spread the dread disease to 5.6 million people in the country. Mandela urged the Mbeki government to allow the lifesaving antiretroviral medicines in public hospitals and clinics.

Mandela's own son Makgatho died in 2005 of complications from AIDS. Immediately Mandela held a press conference to announce the fact. "Let us give publicity to HIV/AIDS," he urged. He meant that it should be regarded as just a disease, not as a secret shame. And it should not be a matter for belief or disbelief, depending on your politics.

In 2004 Mandela joked that he was retiring from his retirement, which so far had been almost as busy as when he was president. This time he really did begin to lead a quieter life. He turned down most invitations and most requests for interviews. Still, he followed world news closely and sometimes even put in a word where he thought he could help. Troubled by human rights abuses in neighboring Zimbabwe, he tried to persuade the president, Robert Mugabe, to step down.

On July 18, 2008, Nelson Mandela's ninetieth birthday, celebrations were held all over South Africa. Mandela himself celebrated in Qunu. He wore one of his colorful silk shirts, and he smiled broadly as his grandchildren sang "Happy Birthday."

Mandela made one last public appearance. When South Africa hosted the soccer World Cup in 2010, Mandela appeared briefly at the closing ceremony. The crowd cheered with delight.

In his last few years, Nelson Mandela was in frail health. He struggled with hearing loss, and he walked with a cane. His eyesight had never recovered from the dust and glare at the quarry on Robben Island. In June 2013 he was hospitalized in critical condition for a lung infection, and he remained in the hospital through July and August.

On December 5, 2013, Nelson Rolihlahla Mandela, of the Madiba clan, died at home in Johannesburg. He was ninety-five. South Africa observed a ten-day period of mourning, including a memorial service at the soccer stadium in Soweto on December 10. In spite of the drenching rain, tens of thousands of South Africans gathered to pay tribute to the father of their country.

Leaders from all over the world joined the crowds in the stadium to pay their respects. President Barack Obama of the United States delivered a eulogy for the "giant of history" who had been a hero and an inspiration to him. "It took a man like Madiba to free not just the prisoner, but the jailer as well," Obama told the South Africans. "Your freedom, your democracy, is his cherished legacy."

Nelson Mandela once said that he was "not a saint, unless you think of a saint as a sinner who keeps on trying." Still, he gave the world an unforgettable moral lesson. Imprisoned for twenty-seven years, he never lost sight of his life's goal: his beloved South Africa as a multiracial democracy. To reach this goal, he kept himself disciplined and worked steadily to keep up his own and his fellow prisoners' spirits. He studied and planned toward that goal.

To Mandela, his attitude was not saintly—only practical. Hating clouds the mind, he pointed out. It gets in the way of strategy. Leaders cannot afford to hate.

So when, miraculously, Mandela found himself president of South Africa, he turned away from the natural impulse of the black majority for revenge. Instead he bent all his efforts to bind the country together and heal the deep wounds of apartheid. Rolihlahla, the troublemaker, had become Madiba, the father of his country.

TIME LINE

July 18, 1918: Born Rolihlahla Mandela in Mvezo, Transkei, South Africa.

1919: Father loses his chieftainship. Mother takes him to live in Qunu.

1925: Begins primary school. He is given his English name, Nelson, by his teacher.

1930: Father dies, and Rolihlahla becomes the ward of Thembu regent, Jongintaba Dalindyebo. Moves to Mqhekezweni and continues his studies at the local mission school.

1934: Undergoes traditional initiation into manhood. Leaves Mqhekezweni for the Clarkebury Boarding Institute in Engcobo.

1937: Progresses to Healdtown, the Wesleyan College at Fort Beaufort.

1939: Enrolls at the University College of Fort Hare, in Alice.

1940: Expelled from Fort Hare.

1941: Mandela and foster brother, Justice, flee to Johannesburg to avoid arranged marriages. Works in gold mine as night watchman. Begins working as law clerk at Witkin, Sidelsky & Eidelman.

1942: Completes BA by correspondence through the University of South Africa. Begins attending African National Congress (ANC) meetings. Regent Jongintaba dies; Mandela visits old homes in the Transkei.

1943: Mandela receives BA from Fort Hare at formal graduation ceremony. Enrolls at the University of Witwatersrand law school. Observes successful boycott of buses from Alexandra to Johannesburg.

1944: Cofounds the Youth League of the ANC. Marries Evelyn Mase.

1945: Son Thembi is born.

1946: Mandela observes black miners' strike.

1947: Daughter Makaziwe is born, to live only nine months.

1948: Mandela elected national secretary of the ANC Youth League. South Africa President Jan Smuts loses to Daniel Malan of the National Party; watershed political turn toward extreme racist policies.

1950: Son Makgatho is born. Government enacts Suppression of Communism Act, Population and Registration Act, Group Areas Act.

1951: Mandela elected president of the ANC Youth League.

1952: Defiance Campaign begins. Mandela arrested, tried, and convicted for "statutory communism"; receives two-year suspended sentence. Elected ANC deputy president. Opens first black South African law firm with partner Oliver Tambo.

1953: Mandela plans for the ANC to go underground in the future.

1954: The Transvaal Law Society tries to remove Mandela's standing as a lawyer. Mandela takes part in protests against planned black population removals from Sophiatown. Daughter Makaziwe is born.

1955: The government evicts black residents from Sophiatown and destroys the buildings. Congress of the People approves the Freedom Charter.

TIME LINE

1956: Mandela and other leaders of the ANC are arrested for "high treason"; pretrial and trial will drag on until 1961.

1957: Evelyn leaves Mandela.

1958: Mandela divorces Evelyn.

June 14, 1958: Marries Winnie Nomzamo Madikizela.

1959: Pan-Africanist Congress breaks off from the ANC. Government passes Promotion of Bantu Self-Government Act.

March 21, 1960: The Sharpeville massacre. Oliver Tambo flees South Africa.

March 30, 1960: Government declares martial law; Mandela is detained.

March 31, 1961: Mandela's trial verdict: not guilty. Mandela goes underground to continue ANC work.

April 8, 1961: The government bans the ANC.

1961: Mandela helps form militant wing of the ANC, "Spear of the Nation," or MK.

January 11, 1962: Mandela leaves South Africa to gather support for the ANC. Travels to conference in Ethiopia; visits several other African nations, as well as London.

July 23, 1962: Returns to South Africa, still underground.

August 6, 1962: Mandela is arrested in KwaZulu.

November 7, 1962: Mandela is sentenced to five years in prison for incitement and leaving the country without a passport.

October 9, 1963: Mandela appears in court for new trial, with new evidence of sabotage from Liliesleaf Farm.

TIME LINE

April 20, 1964: Mandela gives famous "Speech from the Dock."

June 12, 1964: Mandela is sentenced to life imprisonment.

June 13, 1964: Arrives on Robben Island, where he will spend the next eighteen years.

1968: Mother visits Mandela in prison; a few weeks later, she dies.

July 13, 1969: Son Thembi dies in a car accident.

1975: Mandela begins writing autobiography.

June 16, 1976: Uprising in Soweto against "Bantu education"; 176 Africans killed.

September 12, 1977: Steve Biko is murdered by police in prison.

March 31, 1982: Mandela is transferred off Robben Island to Pollsmoor Prison.

May 1984: Mandela is allowed to hold his wife for the first time in twenty-one years.

October 16, 1984: Bishop Desmond Tutu awarded Nobel Prize for peace.

February 10, 1985: Mandela's daughter Zindzi gives his speech in which he rejects President Botha's offer to release him.

1985: Direct contact between Mandela and apartheid government begins with secret visit from Kobie Coetsee, minister of justice.

1988: Talks between the ANC and South Africa's white government begin.

December 7, 1988: Mandela transferred to Victor Verster prison farm.

TIME LINE

August 1989: President Botha resigns; de Klerk becomes president of South Africa. De Klerk begins dismantling apartheid. Political prisoners released.

February 2, 1990: De Klerk's government unbans the ANC.

February 11, 1990: Mandela (age seventy-one) released from prison.

July 5, 1991: Mandela elected ANC president, replacing ailing Oliver Tambo.

December 21, 1991: The racially inclusive Convention for a Democratic South Africa (CODESA) begins.

April 13, 1992: Mandela formally and publicly separates from Winnie.

May 1992: CODESA 2 continues negotiations.

June 17, 1992: Massacre at Boipatong.

August 3, 1992: ANC nationwide strike.

September 7, 1992: Bisho slaughter, Eastern Cape.

February 1993: Transitional government agreed upon.

April 10, 1993: Black leader Chris Hani shot; Mandela prevents violent response by blacks.

April 24, 1993: Oliver Tambo dies.

Fall 1993: Mandela builds his country house in Qunu.

December 10, 1993: Mandela, together with de Klerk, awarded Nobel Peace Prize in Oslo, Norway.

April 27, 1994: First free elections in South Africa. Mandela votes for the first time.

May 10, 1994: Mandela inaugurated as the first black president of South Africa.

TIME LINE

December 14, 1994: Autobiography, *Long Walk to Freedom*, is published.

1995: Mandela establishes the Nelson Mandela Children's Fund. Supports the South Africa Springboks to win World Cup rugby final.

1996: Divorces Winnie Mandela.

July 18, 1998: Marries Graça Machel.

1999: Retires after one term as president. Establishes the Nelson Mandela Foundation.

January 6, 2005: Son Makgatho dies of AIDS.

December 5, 2013: Nelson Mandela dies at home in Johannesburg, age ninety-five.

GLOSSARY

abantu: fellowship

Africanism: the belief that Africa rightfully belongs to black Africans only

Afrikaans: the language, developed from seventeenth-century Dutch, spoken by Afrikaners

Afrikaner: a South African of Dutch heritage

AIDS: a severe immunological disease caused by the retrovirus HIV

apartheid: "apartness," the National Party's system for keeping the races separated

assegai: spear

baas: "boss," a term of submission

ban: to deprive a person of the right of free movement and of association with other persons

Bayete!: "Hail!" A salutation of respect and honor.

Boers: "farmers," the Dutch settlers of South Africa and their descendants

boycott: to protest as a group by refusing to take part, buy, or use

bride-price: a sum of money, cattle, or other valuables, traditionally paid by the groom's family to the bride's family

Ciskei: a Native reserve southwest of the Transkei

civil disobedience: refusal to obey a law, by passive resistance or other nonviolent means

Coloured: a South African term formerly used for mixed-race people

communism: an economic system in which property is held in common and labor is organized for the benefit of all

231

GLOSSARY

Engcobo: a district in the western part of the Transkei

Great Place: the royal residence of the tribal chief

kaffir: an offensive term for a black person

kaross: a traditional tribal cloak

kraal: a fenced enclosure for livestock

labor union: an organization of workers to achieve better wages and working conditions

law clerk: assistant to an attorney, for the purpose of gaining experience in practicing law

liberation movement: an organized effort to achieve equal rights and status

location: a township built by the South African government to house, separate, and control the black population of a city

martial law: temporary rule by military authorities

mass action: action taken by a large number of people, especially the working class or people of low social and economic status

matchbox house: one of thousands of identical, tiny, cheap houses, built by the government to rent to black workers

mealie: corn

mealie pap: corn mush

Mfengu: a tribe driven out of central South Africa by the Zulus

monopoly: control by one group of a product or service

Natal: a region of eastern South Africa on the Indian Ocean

Native: British term for black Africans

"Nkosi Sikelel' iAfrika": "God Bless Africa." The ANC anthem, and, after apartheid, a part of the anthem of South Africa

GLOSSARY

nonviolent disobedience: a tactic of deliberately but peacefully breaking a law, as a means of protest

pass, pass book: an official document that blacks in South Africa, but not whites, were required to carry at all times

passive resistance: resisting a law by nonviolent means, such as demonstrations or marches

praise-singer: one who chants or sings poetry, often to honor heroic deeds

race: an unscientific term to classify people, usually by physical characteristics

racist: a person who believes that differences in ability or character in human beings can be explained by race

removal: mass relocation of black residents against their will

rondavel: a round thatch-roofed hut

sabotage: to undermine, especially by destruction of property

safe house: a house or apartment used as a hiding place by the members of an organization

shebeen: an illegal saloon in a black township

Sotho: the language of the Basotho people, a tribe living in Lesotho, north of the Transkei

stope: a steplike excavation in a mine

strike: a work stoppage by employees, to force employers to consider higher wages or better benefits

Swaziland: a small country between northeastern South Africa and Mozambique, home of the Swazi tribe

Thembu: a Xhosa-speaking tribe of the Eastern Cape of South Africa

Transkei: a Native reserve in southeastern South Africa

GLOSSARY

Transvaal: the northeastern region of South Africa, including the cities of Johannesburg and Pretoria

trek: a slow, difficult journey

ubuntu: the principle that all human beings are connected—that the welfare of a small part of a group, or even of one person, affects everyone

voortrekker: Dutch South African pioneer

white supremacy: the belief that the white or Caucasian race is superior to all other races

Witwatersrand: a rocky ridge in northeastern South Africa with rich deposits of gold ore

Xhosa: the language spoken by a related group of tribes in the Eastern Cape

Zulu: a large tribe of eastern South Africa

SOURCES

BOOKS

Cohen, David Elliot, and John D. Battersby. *Nelson Mandela: A Life in Photographs*. New York: Sterling, 2009.

Cole, Ernest. *House of Bondage*. New York: Random House, 1967.

Lelyveld, Joseph. *Move Your Shadow: South Africa, Black and White*. New York: Times Books, 1985.

Lodge, Tom. *Mandela: A Critical Life*. New York: Oxford University Press, 2006.

Mandela, Nelson. *Long Walk to Freedom: The Autobiography of Nelson Mandela*. Boston: Little, Brown, 1994.

Mandela, Winnie. *Part of My Soul Went with Him*. New York: W. W. Norton, 1985.

Meer, Fatima. *Higher Than Hope: The Authorized Biography of Nelson Mandela*. New York: Harper & Row, 1990.

Meredith, Martin. *Nelson Mandela: A Biography*. New York: St. Martin's Press, 1997.

Paton, Alan. *Cry, the Beloved Country*. New York: Scribners, 1948.

Sampson, Anthony. *Mandela: The Authorized Biography*. New York: Knopf, 1999.

Thompson, Leonard M. *A History of South Africa*. New Haven, CT: Yale University Press, 2000.

PERIODICALS

Dupont, Kevin Paul. "Mandela Started with a Game." *Boston Globe*, December 8, 2013.

SOURCES

Eligon, John. "Hometown Remembers Madiba the Villager, Well Before Mandela the Icon." *New York Times,* December 12, 2013.

Keller, Bill. "Nelson Mandela, 1918–2013." *New York Times,* December 6, 2013.

Molefe, T. O. "Mandela's Unfinished Revolution." *New York Times,* December 15, 2013.

Polgreen, Lydia, and John Eligon. "Thousands Gather for Mandela's Burial." *Boston Globe,* December 16, 2013.

Polgreen, Lydia, and Nicholas Kulish. "Leaders from Across Globe Pay Tribute to Mandela." *Boston Globe,* December 11, 2013.

VIDEO

Cry Freedom (Universal Pictures, Marble Arch, 1987)

Cry, the Beloved Country (Miramax Films, 1995)

Invictus (Warner Bros., 2009)

The Long Walk of Nelson Mandela (PBS Frontline, 1999)

Mandela: Long Walk to Freedom (VideoVision Entertainment, 2013)

Mandela: Son of Africa, Father of a Nation (Palm Pictures, LLC, 2007)

MUSIC

"Nkosi Sikelel' iAfrika," the ANC anthem.
http://www.youtube.com/watch?v=MFW7845XO3g

"Die Stem van Suid-Afrika," the Afrikaner anthem.
http://www.youtube.com/watch?v=e9dq7VqV-Os&

"Free Nelson Mandela," written by Jerry Dammers, performed by the Special AKA, 1984.
http://www.youtube.com/watch?v=AgcTvoWjZJU&feature=kp

SOURCES

INTERNET

Africa Media Online. http://history.africamediaonline.com/home

Apartheid Museum. http://www.apartheidmuseum.org/

Nelson Mandela Foundation. http://www.nelsonmandela.org/

South African History Online. http://www.sahistory.org.za/

UWC-Robben Island Mayibuye Archives. http://www.robben-island.org.za/

Zindzi, Maki, and Zenani Mandela—Nelson Mandela's Daughters
http://dailyentertainmentnews.com/breaking-news/zindzi-maki-and-zenani-mandela-nelson-mandelas-daughters/

INDEX

239

INDEX

INDEX

INDEX

243

INDEX

245

INDEX

INDEX